WM172

Post-Tra

POST-TRAUMA STRESS

Frank Parkinson

sheldon PRESS

First published in Great Britain in 1993
Sheldon Press, SPCK, Marylebone Road, London NW1 4DU

Third impression 1998

Illustration by Alasdair Smith

British Library Cataloguing-in-Publication Data
A catalogue record for this book is available from the
British Library
ISBN 0-85969-662-6

Photoset by Deltatype Ltd, Ellesmere Port, Cheshire
Printed and bound in Great Britain by Biddles Ltd, Guildford and
King's Lynn

No man can hide from his own fears
For they are part of him
And they will always know where he is hiding.

Anon

Contents

| *Preface*

We all experience stress from the moment we are conceived until the day we die and stress is an essential and normal part of our daily lives. It enables us to face the problems of life, problems which sometimes produce further stress and which disrupt the peace and calm we try to seek in what seems to become a more and more hectic world. Stress can be pleasurable when we are riding the 'big-dipper', watching an exciting film or encouraging our team to win. However, dealing with danger and fear in our personal lives, or the lives of those close to us, can produce the 'flight or fight' response when stress enables us either to run away or to stay and face the problem.

There are many situations in life where the stress generated becomes 'dis-stress' and we may find it very difficult to cope. This can be the result of a bereavement, divorce, moving home, being made redundant or some other incident involving change and loss. This stress can then be experienced as post-trauma stress, because the feelings generated at the time of the incident have not gone away, but have become more difficult and distressing. Most people will cope, but some do suffer various disturbing symptoms, not just for a short period of time, but sometimes for the rest of their lives. Our coping mechanisms work, but more successfully for some than for others. However, it must be emphasized that post-traumatic stress reactions are not abnormal or signs of weakness or inadequacy; they are normal responses to abnormal events. Some will react and others will not, but both are normal.

This book is the result of having been involved over a number of years with people who have been through incidents such as accidents, disasters, shootings, bombings, armed robberies, hostage situations, riots, war and other trauma-inducing events. They have been people from the armed forces, the police, prison, fire and rescue and other services, as well as with victims and their families. There are many methods of helping and coping, but the main emphasis of this book is on strategies for coping already used in other situations of loss and, especially, on the model and method used after traumatic incidents known as Psychological

Debriefing or Critical Incident Debriefing. This method has been produced by Atle Dyregrov from Bergen in Norway, following work done by J.T. Mitchell from the United States and others. This method has been used successfully after a number of different incidents and it is suggested that this kind of debriefing should become standard procedure for all organizations and people who experience traumatic events, whether they feel they are suffering or not. This relatively simple procedure needs to be carried out by trained personnel; it will receive the stress and help to prevent the emergence of the deeper and more disturbing symptoms of Post-Traumatic Stress Disorder.

I believe that we all need to be aware of the effects of difficult and traumatic incidents on our lives and on the lives of those around us. Professionally trained counsellors and helpers should be aware of, and can learn the method of, debriefing outlined here. However, I would not recommend in any way that this method of helping be used by those who are not properly trained to do so and who do not meet the criteria outlined later in this book. It is hoped that this material will create further interest in the problems of post-trauma stress and in ways of helping ourselves and others to cope. Stress is with us always and usually we cope; but when we meet a traumatic incident which is outside the range of our normal experiences, our reactions can be painful and deeply disturbing. Even if they are not and we feel that we can cope, talking it through in a structured way with a trained debriefer can be very helpful and encouraging for ourselves, our families and for others involved with us. This method is Psychological, or Critical Incident, Debriefing.

I would like to thank Michael Srinivasan, a psychiatrist, Iris Throp, a social worker, and all those members of the multi-disciplinary team who worked together before and after the Gulf War, for their help, encouragement and friendship. I would like to dedicate this book to them and to the converted, and hope for many more conversions in the future! I would also give my thanks to Janet Johnston of the Dover Counselling Centre, without whom I would not have been introduced to Dyregrov and Mitchell.

Finally, where specific cases are mentioned, these are based on real people and incidents, but in order to protect the identities of those concerned, names and some details have been changed.

Frank Parkinson

1
Introduction

The many disasters of recent years and the release of the hostages held in the Middle East, plus the effects of the war in the Falklands, the conflict in the Gulf and our continuing involvement in Northern Ireland, have all brought sharply into focus the devastating effects these events have had on the lives of many of those involved. Some have been killed and their relatives and friends have suffered the terrible pain and loss of bereavement. Others have been injured or maimed physically and will never be the same again. But there are other injuries which are much more difficult to identify or understand. A broken leg can be painful and incapacitating, but will usually heal. A dreadful and shattering emotional experience can cause problems that may damage people's health, cause the breakdown of relationships, lower the capacity and ability to cope with all areas of life including marriage and work, or be hidden away for many years only to emerge later with even more disturbing effects.

It seems obvious that those at the centre of an accident or disaster, the victims and survivors, will suffer; perhaps less obvious are the possible effects on the rescuers and helpers. Like the ripples on a pond when a stone is thrown into the water, the effects spread out from the centre to include families and friends and many others in an ever-widening circle.

The stresses and reactions produced by traumatic incidents are similar to those of bereavement and grief. This is because experiencing a traumatic incident means loss, and loss is an inevitable consequence of human life, from birth to death. Loss brings change and change can mean growth, but growth is often painful and disturbing. Yet it is the very pain of loss which contains within it the seeds of healing and renewal. Therefore, those who suffer should know that what they are experiencing are normal reactions to abnormal events; the way to renewal and healing is to move through the pain and not deny its existence. To pretend that the pain does not exist or will simply go away can lead to much deeper and more complicated problems at a later stage. There is a need for information, help and support to be made available to those who suffer or are likely to be involved as carers and helpers. The intention of this book is to provide information about the process and nature of traumatic reactions and the connection with loss, and to describe a way of providing support.

In recent years, our understanding of the nature and process of grief and the effects of being involved in traumatic incidents has grown and we are now more able to help others and ourselves to cope. Studies of the effects of disasters and accidents have led to the development of the procedure known as Psychological Debriefing, or Critical Incident Debriefing, and this has been shown to be effective in lessening the possibility of deeper problems emerging at a later stage. This debriefing process is a response by trained personnel, usually two to three days after the event, to people who have been in traumatic incidents. The main focus of the debriefing is on the normalization of reactions and its basis is that those involved are normal people who have experienced an abnormal event. They are not mentally or emotionally sick or ill but are experiencing the normal symptoms of trauma and loss. The process allows them to talk through their experiences in a structured and disciplined way. They are encouraged to move naturally from the facts as they perceive them, to the feelings they had before and during the event. They then look at how they feel now, at what they might need and what resources are available to help them in the future. Some may seek psychiatric or counselling help, but most will be able to cope. Debriefing is for everyone and anyone involved, from victims and survivors to helpers, carers and, in some instances, families. This method and model will be looked at in detail in chapter 7.

Although I was unaware of it at the time, my first involvement in post-trauma stress goes back to my days as a curate in Sunderland in 1962. I called regularly at a particular garage for petrol. One day the man who was serving the petrol had one foot on the bumper of my car and I noticed that there was a livid, red scar around his lower leg. When I asked about this he told me that he had been a prisoner of war in the Far East and had been chained to a wall for long periods of time, hence the mark on his leg. Whenever I called he would talk at great length about his experiences. In retrospect I believe that he needed to talk and that this helped him to come to terms with it. There was no such thing as Psychological Debriefing in those days and he was offered no counselling or help after the war.

After I joined the army, I was asked to help with a number of courses on welfare. These were on general welfare topics such as the purpose of welfare, basic listening skills and bereavement. At that time I saw the need for changes in attitudes towards all welfare problems, including bereavement and loss, and for there to be more training and co-operation between welfare agencies and personnel. My interest in bereavement and loss had grown when I was based in Germany and had to help people to cope with the deaths of babies and young children. The attitudes of many professional helpers and of some in positions of authority appalled me, and I was led by one particular experience of a stillbirth to look at this problem further. All the familiar attitudes were there: 'You'll soon get over it'; 'Put it behind you and have another baby'; 'Look to the future'; 'It's just one of those things that happen'. Even some hospital staff and clergy were content to allow a stillbirth to pass without any kind of formal recognition: without comment; without ritual or burial; without allowing or encouraging the parents to grieve. These experiences made me even more interested in the processes of loss and grief and I became aware, especially through the media, that others were also concerned.

Later I trained as a Relate counsellor, and this was one of the most important and influential experiences of my life. It enabled me to look at myself, but also at the whole field of counselling and helping, and I was able to extend this knowledge and skill into many areas of life.

Following the East Midlands' air crash on the M1 motorway near Kegworth, I was asked to speak to military personnel who had helped at the scene. I had little knowledge of post-trauma stress, but knew something about bereavement, loss and counselling. I had also been involved on a number of occasions with soldiers and their families after the Falklands War and from Northern Ireland. Because of this I was able to conduct a kind of mini-debriefing, although I knew nothing of Dyregrov and Mitchell. My aim was to get those involved to talk by giving a presentation on loss and stress, to reassure them that their reactions were normal and that they were not weak or inadequate if they experienced unusual reactions. Many of the women found it easy to talk, but the men generally felt unable to do so. How I wish I had known about Psychological Debriefing.

I was then asked to help the prison chaplaincy team after the

Strangeways riots in Manchester. I contacted Janet Johnston from the Dover Counselling Centre to ask her advice. She asked about my professional training and experiences and then said that she would send me some information about a method of helping called Psychological Debriefing. She encouraged me to look at this and assured me that it would help. This was my introduction to the work of Atle Dyregrov and J. T. Mitchell. I spent two days with the chaplaincy team in a retreat house on the edge of the Pennines and used the model she had sent me. It was such a moving and stimulating experience that I wrote to Dr Dyregrov in Norway and he was kind enough to show an interest in my work and encouraged me to use and adapt his model.

After the invasion of Kuwait, and before the Gulf War broke out, I visited the military help-line set up in London for the families and relatives of those held hostage in Kuwait and Iraq. I suggested that on their return they would need Psychological Debriefing and, somewhat to my surprise, this was accepted by the Ministry of Defence. This was organized first for the wives who returned and, later, for the men. Some young adults and children were also involved. More of this is discussed later in this chapter. However, I became even more convinced that those who experience trauma need much more than what is now called 'defusing': help and encouragement at the time of the incident and shortly after. Psychological Debriefing will help them to come to terms with their experiences and lessen the possibility of deeper psychological problems emerging later.

Also, at this time, a group of soldiers were being trained for the Army Graves' Registration Team for the Gulf War with the expectation that there could be large numbers of casualties. I was asked if I would help, so I took a morning with these men and encouraged them to look at all their anxieties and worries. I was quite surprised that when asked to discuss this in small groups, they were able to produce an almost text-book set of responses. It was all there: concern for their families at home; fear of dying and of combat; the desire to do the best for the dead and their relatives. Would they be able to cope? What about the macho image they were meant to show? Would they be able to deal with the dead bodies? How would they react? Would it become easier or more difficult? How would they cope if the dead were known to them? Would they make mistakes? Would they cope with the heat and periods of boredom? Would they be able to sleep and rest? How would it affect them when they returned home? What would be the effects on their families? Theirs would be a difficult and distressing task, and they knew it. On their return from the Gulf and at the request of their commanding officer, Psychological Debriefing was carried out by members of the same team who had debriefed the Gulf hostages.

Because of this involvement and experience, I was asked to help people after car accidents and other traumatic incidents. This spread into the civilian world and the local police invited me to help people who were suffering trauma after various incidents including a fatal shooting and a violent family hostage situation. There was little available to help except to refer them to a psychiatrist, clinical psychologist or counsellor, many of whom knew little about the problems of post-trauma stress or of the method of helping through Psychological Debriefing. My next involvements were with personnel following bank and building society armed robberies and, at the request of medical staff, with some survivors of the Baltic Exchange bombings in London.

More recently, I was asked by the social services to look at the problem of stress for social work staff in a particular area of a county. Perhaps not surprisingly, I found that most just wanted to talk, but also that the strategies they used for coping with the stress of their work were identical to those used by helpers in disaster situations. It seems that trauma produces similar coping mechanisms in people, whatever the situation might be.

All these experiences have convinced me that normal counselling is not sufficient to help those who suffer from post-trauma stress. The process of Psychological Debriefing should be an essential element in our response to victims and helpers after traumatic incidents. All that is needed is knowledge of post-trauma stress and its effects and influences on those involved and a group of counsellors trained in the Dyregrov and Mitchell method and model. Psychological Debriefing could and should be written into the standard response of organizations and institutions such as the armed forces, police, fire and rescue services, banks, building societies, hospitals and medical services. It all seems so simple. But this is not the case, for there is a basic resistance in many people and organizations to any kind of helping response other than 'defusing' and counselling. Counselling can help, but Psychological Debriefing is far more effective and the benefits for all would be enormous.

When the invasion of Kuwait took place in August 1990, a large number of individuals and families from the United Kingdom and other countries were held hostage. At that time, some members of a closely-knit team of over eighty families based in Kuwait were on holiday away from the Gulf and they immediately set up a helpline in London for relatives and families back home. Amongst these helpers, there were feelings of guilt and regret that they were not with their friends when the crisis broke out. They felt a great deal of anxiety and concern, not only about their friends in Kuwait and Iraq, but also because their own homes were there. They had left irreplaceable personal belongings behind and their lives were still focused with their friends and colleagues in the Gulf. They had lost their homes, places of work, their community and also personal possessions, some of which were of deep sentimental value. One man expressed this simply when he said that it felt awful to think that strangers were looking at photographs of his daughter. There was also great concern for their Kuwaiti friends and neighbours. Running this network provided an essential service for the relatives of the families at home but it also met a deep need for those who were running the helpline. They felt useful and needed, were kept informed about whatever was happening and were in constant touch with anxious and worried relatives of the hostages.

At a later stage, most of the wives and children were allowed to come home, although a few opted to stay with their husbands. A multidisciplinary team was created to carry out psychological debriefing on their return. This team consisted of chaplains, social workers, welfare assistants, hospital welfare personnel, two psychiatrists and a clinical psychologist, all of whom had extensive experience of counselling and group work. They met together to train and carried out debriefing on the return of the hostages. Those who had been running the helpline were included.

Some of the hostages coped afterwards by keeping in touch, especially by telephone. They contacted each other regularly and provided a wide network of support and information. Most attended the voluntary debriefings which also included sessions giving advice and help about housing, finance and insurance. However, not everybody felt able to take part. For some, there was a sense of intense isolation and they did not want to be in contact with others, even with those who were their close friends.

A few were unable to do things such as filling in forms or making even simple decisions, and because of their feelings of anger, disorientation, confusion, loneliness and the separation from their husbands, a few thought they were going mad. Some also felt a strong resistance to the debriefing process and said that they didn't want to be counselled. This was partly the result of the powerful defence of denial which will be discussed later. The fact that debriefing was not counselling was irrelevant. They felt vulnerable and threatened. This was the first time that debriefing had been carried out under such circumstances in the army. Debriefing was not seen as part of the normal response to crisis and some thought it was only for those who acknowledged that they were suffering or who showed signs of distress. Part of the thesis of this book is that debriefing should not be an optional extra and a luxury for a select few or for those who are overtly in need. It is for all those involved, victims and helpers alike, and should be standard procedure whenever there is a crisis or traumatic incident.

This was expressed by some of the hostages when they were offered psychological debriefing:

'When we landed, we expected a medical and a normal debriefing, but we also needed someone to talk to about what we had been through and how we felt. We got the first two, but not the third, until now.'

There were many different reactions from those involved. Amongst the wives who returned early, impulsive actions were not unusual.

June's husband was a hostage and she said that when he was released and came home she would meet him at the airport. She would go and hire an expensive car, perhaps a Porsche or Maserati, and park it outside the airport. When her husband stepped off the plane she would hug and kiss him and then take him outside and say, 'There you are love, I've sold the house and spent all our money on a car for you.' She said she was joking, but there was an element of truth behind it. She too was going through trauma and loss and had a strong desire to do something extravagant for her husband when he returned. It was an impulsive statement which expressed her elation at the prospect of her ordeal, and that of her husband, coming to an end, but it also said a great deal about her anxiety, fear and sense of loss. Fortunately, she didn't carry out her threat for I dread to think of her husband's reactions had she done so!

Many wives had strong feelings of guilt and extreme anger and blamed themselves, anyone and everyone, because the situation had been allowed to happen in the first place and because they had left their husbands behind. One further element was the uncertainty about the outcome in the Gulf and, for the wives, underneath all the feelings was the possibility that they might never see their husbands again. Fortunately this did not happen and the men were eventually allowed to come home just before the war broke out.

Similarly, some soldiers who were left behind by units who went to the Gulf often felt guilty and frustrated that they were not with their friends, even though they knew they were performing an essential task in caring for the families of those who had gone. Some wanted to be there because this was where they felt a sense of belonging and comradeship. In addition to this, if some of their friends were killed, they would feel even more guilty about having stayed behind.

In this situation, anger, frustration, blame and guilt were all typical symptoms.

Such feelings are not confined to hostage situations or war. Riots can produce powerful feelings of anger and frustration on the part of those who are there as helpers and carers. A clergyman who was involved in a riot received many letters of support from Christian groups throughout the country. They said they were praying for him and thinking about him. During the debriefing after the event, when discussing anger, he said,

'I was glad about their support, but some of the letters made me so angry that I could have hit the people who wrote them. Many quoted the verse from the New Testament which says that for those who love God everything works for good (Romans 8. v28). This made me angry in two ways. First, because in the midst of the turmoil, destruction and fear of the event, I did not feel that it was relevant and it didn't help. They didn't understand what was happening and how devastated I felt. Second, I was angry because for years I have used the same quotation myself to others. . . .'

This clergyman had come to look at his faith in a new light, and this would influence the way he responded to people in distress. Some lose their faith completely and others find it.

The curate visited a house at random and a woman came to the door who said: 'I'll not invite you in because I am not a Christian. I was, but I lost my faith when I served as a nurse in the Spanish Civil War. I saw such terrible things and if people can treat each other like that there can't be a God.'

However, in the same parish there was a man in the church choir who had been a regular member since the Second World War. He often said that before the war he didn't have a faith, but he saw such inhumanity and suffering during the war that he came to believe there must be something better, and so found Christianity.

Similar experiences of traumatic events can have very different effects. Some seem to need others whilst a few feel a sense of isolation and loneliness and want to be on their own. Some lose faith and others find it, and many who experience tragedy and trauma in their lives and the lives of those around them often ask questions about meaning and purpose.

- What's the point and purpose of life?
- Is there any reason to live and is the world a good place to live in?
- Are there such things as justice and truth?
- Is life fair?
- Does God exist and, if so, what is this God like?
- Why do awful things happen to people who don't deserve it – or perhaps they do?
- Why did this happen to me and my family?
- Why is life like this?

Some will come to believe that there is no point and no God and that life is not worth living. A few might be so desolate that they lose the will to carry on. The answer, if there is one, lies in suicide. There is no point in anything any more and nothing to live for.

Others find faith in atheism or humanism, or reject any kind of orthodox belief. Others turn to religion or seek answers and comfort in spiritualism and mysticism. Some have difficulty in making simple decisions.

Ted was a policeman and came home in the middle of a riot that had lasted a few days and was likely to continue. As he walked into the house his wife spoke to him: 'Hello love. What would you like for supper, fish-fingers and chips or beefburgers and chips?' Ted couldn't cope with this and was unable to decide. Not only that, he became very angry and shouted: 'What the hell does it matter anyway?' He said later that he was going through such turmoil in his mind and was surrounded by so much violence and hatred that the question was trivial beyond words. 'I'm going through this,' he said, 'and she asks me that!'

A soldier who returned from the Gulf said:

'I could not settle down, and making simple decisions was difficult. Even getting out of bed and making the effort to go to work was almost more than I could manage. Throughout the day I felt listless and tired and just couldn't be bothered with anything or anyone. Everything was just too much trouble for me.'

Another common response to crisis and disaster is that things that were once very important can become irrelevant.

'If you have a lovely home and your family have been killed in a disaster, then it doesn't seem to matter any more. The people who made it a home rather than a house have gone. Material things become unimportant. After all, they are only things and not people. Also, there is no real value or sense in having status in life, a job or in achieving and succeeding. What is this for if you are now on your own and have lost those you love?'

The opposite of this can happen. Things that were perhaps not very important or were taken for granted, particularly objects, can assume a value seemingly out of all proportion to their worth. In particular, buildings can become the focus of people's emotions and feelings. This was true in the Manchester prison riots where the prison building was seen by some not just as a place of work, but endowed with almost human characteristics and personality. It was a closely-knit community of people, like a walled town.

When this was mentioned to Dr Atle Dyregrov, an expert on post-trauma stress based in Norway, he wrote in a letter in February 1991:

> I was struck by the phenomenon that you mention, and that I have noticed in several of the disasters that I have worked with, namely how material objects can have a very strong symbolic value. I remember vividly from my work with the California earthquake in 1989 how the inhabitants of Santa Cruz described the enormous emotional effect it had on them that the Mall had been destroyed. This Mall was the centre of so many sentiments in the city, and its destruction meant that parts of their lives were destroyed. In disaster workers it is often not the destruction and mutilation of a human body that strikes them hardest, but seeing a child's toy or some other symbolic object that brings the personal ramifications of the event close (Personal letter of 1 Feb. 1991 from Dr Atle Dyregrov, Bergen, Norway.)

Those who lose their homes in a disaster can have similar responses. Buildings, toys, shoes and other objects can be the focus of our emotions for they remind us very starkly what the event has cost in terms of human and personal suffering. Perhaps the nearest to this in other areas is the importance of a ship to the crew who see it not just as an object but refer to it as 'she', as though it was human. Its loss and sinking can have a devastating effect upon them. A regiment in the army, its flag or standard and its tradition, can have a similar personal identity and some will mourn the loss of their battalion, regiment or corps in a war or in any changes which take place through military restructuring. Breaking this powerful sense of attachment to objects or closely-knit groups can evoke very strong feelings of loss.

This can also apply in cases where communities rely on a factory, coal mine, shipyard, shop, store or other industry for their welfare. People often identify very strongly with their place of work and the closing down of an industry is a disaster which can bring a deep sense of personal loss for those involved. Bricks and mortar become humanized and identified as the focus for feelings of acute and painful loss. This can be extended to the experiences of redundancy and unemployment, which may also result in trauma and feelings of rejection and loss.

Some or all of these symptoms can be experienced in what might be seen as minor events when compared with major disasters. Car accidents, accidents at work, having an operation, being made redundant, a divorce or separation, moving house, being involved in violence, witnessing a traumatic incident – all can result in guilt and anger, isolation and loneliness, vulnerability and depression, loss of faith and self-worth, changes in values and attitudes, fear and shame, nightmares and sleep disturbances, marital breakdown and illness, self-blame and bitterness. All of these are symptoms of loss and trauma.

Basic Beliefs

The experience of loss causes the disruption of the basic beliefs and feelings we have grown to accept throughout our lives so that they have become part of our agenda and expectation. It is as though we have a huge pack on our backs which is gradually being filled with experiences as we grow and develop. When we face any situation, we reach into the pack for the tools we need in order to cope. Some of these tools are the beliefs we have absorbed, and we build ourselves and the pattern of our lives around them until they are disturbed or we find they don't seem to fit the situation or our needs. There are three basic beliefs which we all accept in some measure and have put into our packs as tools.

1   Invulnerability

We tend to think that life is fairly safe and secure: 'Bad things happen to other people and not to me.' Our general experience of life is that most of us do survive without being involved in any major accidents or disasters and our very strong defence mechanisms are there to protect us from becoming over anxious. We live our lives as optimists, in the false belief that we will live forever and that harm or danger will not touch us.

When we are suddenly confronted by a traumatic and shattering experience our safe little world can collapse and be turned upside down, resulting in confusion and fear.

- 'Your wife has left you for another man.'
- 'I'm sorry, your husband has had a heart-attack at work.'
- 'You have cancer and about six months to live.'

Other experiences can have similar effects, such as being a survivor in a car crash, accident or disaster, being raped, violently assaulted or held hostage, witnessing or being involved in violence, war, murder, suicide, shootings or robberies. All of these make us aware that we are not invulnerable. We are mortal. We can die. Life is not secure or safe; it is uncertain and sometimes appears to be the result of malevolent and impersonal forces. These experiences can cause intense fear and anxiety as well as the loss of security and confidence in self, others or life in general.

2 Meaning and purpose

Most of the time we feel that we have a reason to live and carry on. Meaning and purpose can come from happy and satisfying relationships, a good job, achieving success and from the firm belief that life makes sense. It might even come from religious belief. Incidents and experiences which induce trauma and stress call into question this basic belief.

If your child is killed or dies, then your life has been devastated. There isn't any meaning or purpose in it. Similarly, if you are involved in an accident or disaster, your world can be shattered. Life loses its meaning when such tragedies occur and any purpose you thought there was in living is called into question. Similarly, if you are involved in war and conflict where you see death and destruction close at hand, or your life is threatened and you think you are going to die, then you can wonder what all this is for and if there is any sense or reason behind it. This can cause intense and overwhelming fear, anger and frustration, and the desire to scream at the universe about the total injustice of life.

The result of these disturbances can be the loss of any sense of purpose in living and lead to the conclusion that life is without meaning, a sick joke and an utter waste of time. In some cases this can result in depression, a sense of pointlessness and even suicide.

3 Self-respect

Most people have a reasonably positive image of themselves and believe that they are fairly good and decent citizens who, in difficult circumstances, would do whatever they could to help others. Therefore we can build up a strong image of ourselves where we have developed a sense of self-worth and self-esteem.

Difficult experiences can harm or destroy these images. Those involved in an accident where others are killed or injured can feel that they might have acted differently. 'Perhaps I could have saved somebody's life?' 'If only I'd left home ten minutes later, then this would not have happened.'

We can lose our sense of dignity and worth and feel guilt, anger, regret, resentment and bitterness. The foundations of our world begin to crumble and the ground begins to shake under our feet. We begin to question our own self-worth and value as a human being.

The symptoms which can follow the destruction or questioning of the basic foundations of our life beliefs are similar to those of bereavement and grief. We are *shocked*; we feel a great sense of *anger*; we become *depressed* and lose any belief that we can carry on. These are compounded by other feelings which can accompany them – unreality, numbness, guilt and blame, regret and rejection, helplessness and loss of purpose, isolation and loneliness, loss of identity and meaning. Hopefully, given time, most of us will be able to work through the pain and come to healing. With patience, help and understanding we can rediscover a sense of purpose in our lives and slowly renew our feelings of self-worth.

The problem is that it can be a long and painful process and, because of this, it is necessary for both victims and helpers to be aware of the nature and symptoms of post-trauma stress so they know what is happening to them and why. Also, they need to know what can be done to help them.

We have looked at some of the results of trauma and stress; we will go on to examine the symptoms in more detail so that we can understand how widely they can affect people and what can happen to those involved. We shall look at loss as a common experience in human life and its connection with traumatic reactions. We shall also examine the involvement and experiences of helpers. Finally, we consider the method and model of psychological debriefing as a normal response to those involved in trauma, and how it can help them come to terms with their experiences and so cope better with their lives.

2
What is Post-Trauma Stress?

Any incident we experience which is sudden and unexpected can result in emotional as well as physical trauma and shock. This emotional shock can cause stress reactions which are identified as Post-Trauma Stress or Critical Incident Stress. This kind of stress therefore results from experiencing a traumatic incident and can be the result of anything from a slight accident to involvement in a major disaster.

> Billy, aged 4, has fallen off his bicycle and runs to his mother crying. He has bruised both his knees as well as his pride. His mother puts her arms around him, comforts him and asks what has happened. He sobs out his story. He was riding down the path on his new bike when suddenly the front wheel slipped and he crashed onto the ground. He has hurt his knee and his bike is still lying where it fell. He is sobbing gently in his mother's arms, breathing in short gasps. He tells her that it's a rotten bike anyway and it was the bike's fault and he's never going to ride it again, ever! His mother holds him and tells him that he'll be all right. She will go with him to get his bike and bring it home and then he can ride it again when he feels better. She puts some ointment on his knees and some tender loving care on his pride and gradually he stops crying. She takes his hand and they both go outside and collect the bike. He is frightened at first, but with her beside him holding the seat, he climbs onto it again and slowly pedals down the pathway wobbling from side to side.

A simple incident, but one which is a major step in Billy's life. He is shocked and crying, runs to his mother for help and comfort, tells her his story and she helps him to have the confidence to ride his bicycle again. He is suffering from physical pain and from the mental and emotional shock and stress caused by the unexpected fall. If his mother had told him not to be stupid and had not offered him any comfort, but had forced him to 'get out there and be a man', he would either have been put off bikes for the rest of his life or gritted his teeth and climbed back on again. However, his mother might have taken a different approach: 'Don't worry about that nasty little bike. Just leave it there in the road and when Daddy comes home he'll get rid of it. Tomorrow we'll get you a nice football. That can't hurt you.'

Billy's reaction to any of these responses from his mother could have been very different. He might have buried his fears away, had dreams or nightmares about the fall, kept away from bicycles for ever and cried or shouted out with fear whenever he came near one. Equally well, he could cope by forcing himself to conquer his fear, but this fear could have emerged in some other way either at the time or later.

This is an exaggerated example, but even a relatively simple incident can cause reactions of stress and trauma. Billy has experienced some of the typical symptoms of post-trauma stress – shock, pain, fear, crying, blaming, avoidance, and the need for help and comfort.

A traumatic incident can be far more serious than falling off a bicycle.

Andy was driving his car very carefully down the motorway at a steady 60 miles per hour. It was almost midnight and he was on his way back home from a party at a friend's house 50 miles away. Jim, his best friend, was in the front passenger seat asleep. Andy knew that Jim was feeling excited because he was meeting his girlfriend the next day. She was at college and he had not seen her for four weeks. It was slightly foggy and Andy was driving with great care. Suddenly he saw a bright light flash into his eyes and there was a loud bang. The next thing he knew he was spinning around in the car. There was a second loud noise and the car stopped with a crash. He was dazed for a few seconds, but managed to open the door of the car and stagger out. He felt that he must get away from the danger. There was blood on his face and his left arm was hanging by his side. He saw a car behind him and the driver came forward and asked if he could help. They looked into the car and found that Jim was obviously dead. Within minutes the police and an ambulance arrived and Andy was taken to hospital where he was found to be suffering from a broken arm, concussion and severe cuts and bruises to the head. Because he was also suffering from shock, he was kept in hospital for over a week and then sent home where he was back at work in the factory within a fortnight.

His boss found that Andy was acting rather strangely. He couldn't concentrate and sometimes just stared vacantly into space. He talked about not sleeping and when he did he had nightmares. He even thought he saw Jim looking at him through a window in the factory office and in the rear-view mirror of his car. His boss told him to go home and see the doctor.

While he was in hospital he had been visited regularly by a doctor and the chaplain. They both told him that it had been a terrible accident, but he must remember that he was not to blame. A man had been driving down the wrong side of the motorway and had hit his car almost head-on. Jim had been killed because he had not been wearing his seat-belt. Andy had known about the seat-belt, but had not said anything at the time because Jim was relaxing and asleep. In hospital, Andy was very distressed, not only because of the shock, but because of Jim's death and because he had not been able to attend the funeral. The doctor told him that he would be all right and that although it was a tragedy he should put it behind him and remember that it wasn't his fault. Other members of staff told him the same. Over a month later he went to his local GP. Unfortunately the doctor didn't know much about this kind of condition and gave him anti-depressants.

Many doctors, hospital staff, clergy, social workers, counsellors and other helpers do not understand post-trauma stress and there is sometimes the belief, as with bereavement, that people will 'soon get over it' and be back to normal within a relatively short time. There is still a common attitude that such experiences, no matter how traumatic and difficult, can be dealt with quite simply by not letting them get you down. 'Keep a stiff upper lip and carry on with life.' 'When the going gets tough, the tough get going.' The attitude is that all you need to do is put it out of your mind and just get on with your life.

We have either forgotten or do not know that when we experience something that is horrific, intensely disturbing, or shocking and painful, it does not go away. It becomes part of our experience and can result in many disturbing and frightening symptoms, especially if we do not acknowledge these and deny their existence. The feelings and emotions become buried away in our minds and lie there slowly affecting all around them, waiting for the opportunity to emerge and influence other areas of our lives.

Most of us are not tough enough to face the disasters and losses which come to us because we have never faced them or experienced them before. The resulting symptoms can be extremely disturbing, even disabling, and might destroy our lives so that we cannot cope, our families and friends cannot cope with us, our marriages break down, we are unable to work, and our health begins to suffer. Only in relatively recent years have we begun to study and understand the symptoms we now call post-trauma stress, although they have been identified and known for many years under different names.

Shell-shock

During World War One there was a condition known generally as 'shell-shock' in the belief that it was induced by the explosions of shells on the battlefield. The resulting symptoms were many and disturbing: twitching and shaking of limbs, catatonic states, inability to sleep or relax, manic behaviour, depression, loss of speech and memory, and even paralysis.

> A schoolboy story I remember from the 1950s told of an officer in the Great War who suffered from paralysis of the right hand and was invalided out of the front line, whereupon his condition improved. Every time he went back into the line, the condition appeared again. The explanation given was that when troops went 'over the top', they were led by an officer who normally carried a pistol in his right hand. This man's fear was so great that he repressed it, but it surfaced as a psychosomatic reaction where his right hand was immobilized. If he couldn't use his right hand, then he couldn't go with his men into battle. He was dealing with his fear by pushing it down into his mind, but he could not prevent it from emerging as a physical symptom, even though he was unaware of the cause.

Perhaps this was an apocryphal story, but it contains the seeds of truth about the probable causes of the condition known as shell-shock – intense fear, the desire to run away and escape, the belief that this was not the done thing, the sights and sounds of the battlefield, plus the horror and experience, or imminence, of battle. Probably some of the men who were shot as deserters or labelled as cowards were suffering from post-trauma stress. Many of these deserters did not show any physical signs of illness except that they were extremely frightened and had run away. Some who suffered symptoms of stress did receive understanding and treatment, but it seems that in such circumstances as the terror and carnage of the First World War there was little sympathy for those who 'funked it'. Almost every home was affected and the sheer numbers of casualties were unimaginable. On the first day of the Battle of the Somme there were sixty thousand killed or injured. Little wonder that those who were unable to cope were often despised, treated as deserters and, on some occasions, executed. There were, however, some who were more enlightened. One chaplain writing home from the front said:

'No words can tell you how I feel, nor can words tell you of the horrors of the clearing of a battlefield. This Battalion was left to do just that and several men went off with shell-shock and two more were wounded. I am certain the shell-shock was caused not just by the explosion of shells nearby, but by the sight, smell and horror of the battlefield in general. I felt dreadful.'

He believed that this condition was due to the sheer horror induced by the total experience of being on the battlefield – the fear and terror, the noise of explosions and the screams of men, the smells and sights, the carnage, the bodies, the mud and blood and the death and destruction of war. For him, these were the causes of shell-shock.

Battle-stress

Eventually shell-shock became known as 'battle-shock', 'battle-fatigue', 'combat-fatigue' or 'battle-stress', and was recognized as a specific reaction to war and conflict. In the Second World War, when it was possible, troops were given periods of rest and even leave. Some air crews were allowed to fly only a certain number of missions before they were relieved of duty and to this day soldiers in Northern Ireland serving on short tours of duty are given 'R & R', rest and recreation, in the middle of their tour. This recognizes that they need a break, that they need to see their families and the families need to see them. It is intended to reduce the strain and stress for all concerned and lessen the likelihood of problems arising.

The American experience in Vietnam was a major step forward in our understanding of what can happen to men on the battlefield and afterwards. In the preparation of their soldiers for combat, the Americans included training sessions on the possible psychological effects of war and combat. Some claim that this significantly reduced the number of psychological casualties. However, when the men did not return home there was a general reluctance to accept them or to see them as heroes fighting in a just war, and this compounded the problems. Some of the soldiers responded with feelings of intense anger and frustration and suffered the trauma of mental breakdown. Some were unable to take or retain a job; others could not make or keep stable relationships and their marriages broke down. There were feelings of anger, bitterness and guilt, and some blamed themselves for what had happened. Some dropped out of 'normal' society and formed communes or lived in isolation, whilst others could see no point in living and committed suicide.

There were emotional and psychological casualties from earlier wars where the symptoms were not quite so obvious.

Dennis had been a soldier in the Second World War and this seemed to be the high point of his life. He could talk about nothing else. If you said, 'What a lovely day. Just look at the sun shining on those trees', he would say, 'Yes, I remember it was just like that when we were outside Paris – it was a Thursday, no it was Tuesday because that German Messerschmitt came over, and we were in this orchard and my mate had caught some chickens and we were going to have them for dinner and this officer came over and told us to go down to the crossroads to see if it was clear and when we got there we saw some soldiers on the other side of this gully and I said that they were our lads, but my mate said they didn't look like them and then we saw they were Germans so we ran back to the camp and thought that we weren't going to be dead heroes and when we got back we saw this cow in a field and decided to have steak for supper and there was this ruined house and. . . .'

He never fails to tell you a long and complicated story, no matter what you say to him, so people avoid talking to him. He finds difficulty in facing the world of today, and continually lives in the past.

Part of the problem for Dennis is that he talks constantly about things that are either humorous or general – never about any disturbing events such as the death of friends or his experience of battle. Uncle Albert from 'Only Fools and Horses' on the television is an old sailor who receives similar treatment from his friends, Del-boy and Rodney. He bores them to death with his war stories on the few occasions when they give him the chance. If Dennis felt able to talk about the more difficult and disturbing things he experienced, then he might find that he could begin to come to terms with his feelings. Also, he might discover that he has less need to talk and would be able to live more in the present.

Unlike Dennis, some are unable to talk and they bury their experiences deep inside and try to cover them up. The problem is that they can emerge many years later.

Andrew was 66 years old and a business man who worked one evening a week as a volunteer helper for a local organization. He was attending a course on bereavement and stress to help with his work. The lecturer was showing them a video about the Falklands' conflict where a young soldier was talking about burying the dead. The lecturer noticed that Andrew was looking at the floor and thought that he must be bored or uninterested. After the session they had a break for coffee and Andrew came up to him and said, 'I'm sorry about that. You probably thought I was being rude, but I was a young medic in France during the last war and my unit was attacked by an enemy fighter. Afterwards I had to help to pick up and bury what was left of some of my friends. I was terrified at the time and we never talked about it. I had to do this a number of times. I know now that this has been with me for over 45 years hovering in the back of my mind and I've never come to terms with it. I need help. I need someone to talk to.'

Coping with battle-stress

Many modern armies have strategies for helping people to cope with battle-stress. This method can be called 'The 5 Rs' because it involves Removal, Rest, Recounting, Reassurance and Return.

- *Removal* Once symptoms have been recognized, the soldier is moved to a position not far behind the front line. It is essential that he should not be evacuated or treated as someone who is ill or sick. He is not hospitalized or made into a patient and the stress is on the normality of his reactions. He is allowed to keep his uniform, combat kit and weapons so that he remains a soldier on duty and not a patient in pyjamas. Also, where possible, he is kept in touch with his friends and comrades and made aware of what's happening to them.

- *Rest* The soldier is allowed time to rest and relax, as far as he is able, and this is helped by his removal from the noise and confusion of the front. He may also be able to sleep or perform light duties, especially where he is helping others and feels useful.

- *Recounting* The soldier is encouraged to talk about what has been happening to him and hopefully he is able to speak about his feelings and anxieties. This should be done with someone who takes an uncritical and non-judgemental attitude towards him. He is seen and treated as a normal soldier temporarily affected by what he has experienced around and within him; talking helps him to bring out his fears and face them in a supportive environment.

- *Reassurance* One major fear is that such reactions might suggest to a soldier that he is a coward or a failure, is going mad or is letting down his friends and unit or that he is weak or suffering from what was once called 'LMF': lack of moral fibre! He is given assurance that he is not weak or wet or having a nervous breakdown, that his reactions are normal, and that he will soon be back with his comrades. This reassurance of the normality of his reactions and feelings is essential.

- *Return* After a relatively short period of time the soldier should be able to return to duty with his unit and carry on as normal. When he does return, he goes back to his usual duties and is expected to carry on with his work surrounded by the familiarity, friendship and support of his comrades.

This process could include another R – *Recovery* – for if the procedure is successful, he will fully recover. The overriding emphasis is placed on treating him as a human being, someone who is experiencing normal reactions to abnormal events; he is not a coward, wimpish or weak.

Similar strategies are used by therapists, counsellors and psychiatrists when dealing with certain conditions in individuals or in family therapy. This is mentioned by John Cleese and Robin

Skynner in chapter 2 of their book, *Families and How to Survive Them*. Robin Skynner speaks of everyone having an internal 'mental map' of their world (page 68ff); when something traumatic happens this map has to be changed and adjusted. He explains that in order to adjust we need:

Rest – time off and space to breathe;
Reassurance – that all will be well;
Emotional support – someone just being there with us.

This is similar to the method described above used to help soldiers suffering from battle-stress or combat-fatigue and it can be usefully applied to all occasions when we are faced with sudden change or trauma.

This method of treating traumatic symptoms gives us a clue about how to define post-trauma stress. It is the reactions experienced from being involved in a traumatic incident, such as a sudden shock, a death in the family, or witnessing an accident or disaster, or an ongoing experience such as a war or being held hostage. The symptoms of post-trauma stress can also be found before the incident is over. A soldier on the battlefield is not necessarily suffering from 'post'-trauma stress, but has to endure constant stress, perhaps over a long period of time. He might suffer during the battle, but control his emotions and feelings, or he might develop and show symptoms and receive help. However, it is afterwards, when he moves from the field of battle, or when the battle is over and he returns home, that he might suffer from post-traumatic stress reactions. Similarly, those involved in accidents or disasters as helpers might find themselves undergoing stress whilst carrying out their duties and further stress later when they leave the scene.

In the current climate, there is an enormous industry surrounding the whole problem of stress in our society. There are relaxation tapes and videos, classes to attend, yoga, meditation techniques, books and pamphlets – all to help people learn to relax and cope with the pressures of modern living. Events of recent years, especially following traumatic incidents, have also brought the problems of coping with stress sharply into focus.

We have seen the Falklands War (1982) and Gulf War (1990), and the many disasters such as Zeebrugge (March 1987), the King's Cross fire (November 1987), Piper Alpha (July 1988),

Hillsborough (April 1989), air and train crashes, fires, bombings and shootings, and the traumas caused by acts of terrorism and murder.

Disasters affect people other than those immediately involved. The return of the hostages from the Middle East has shown how their incarceration has affected their families and friends. Brian Keenan, John McCarthy, Jackie Mann, Terry Waite and many others have been seen and interviewed on television and in the media. Their faces alone have spoken volumes about how they have been affected by their experiences of isolation and, sometimes, brutal or violent treatment. These people have endured something beyond our imagination and they will probably find difficulty in coming to terms with their experiences. They suffered physical and mental stresses which will not go away just because they have returned home. They have to adjust to their new freedom and relate to the many changes that have taken place in themselves, in their families and friends and in the world around them. Their stress is of a particular kind in that it was something they experienced over a long period of time. It was not the sharp or sudden shock of an accident or disaster. In some cases the reactions have been extremely intense and disturbing whilst others appear to have coped quite well, but they will still, to a greater or lesser degree, suffer some of the symptoms typical of post-trauma stress.

Post-trauma stress: a definition

What then is post-trauma stress? At its simplest it can be defined as 'The normal reactions of normal people to events which, for them, are unusual or abnormal'. However, the problem arises as to which events, for us, are unusual or abnormal. For most of us it is not normal to be involved in a disaster or accident or to have our lives threatened; the effects of such incidents on the human mind and body can be quite dramatic and traumatic. We do not expect to face sudden shock or trauma: the car, aeroplane or train crash; the hooded gunman shouting or screaming at us; ourselves lying in the gutter, beaten up and robbed by thugs. Even when we are trained to do a difficult job the effects can still be traumatic. The police marksman or soldier trained to shoot at people, the fireman or doctor, can still be traumatized by what they see and sometimes have to do. All of these incidents, and many more, can result in some of the symptoms of post-trauma stress. This applies not only to those who are victims or survivors, but also to their families, to those who are called in to help, and even onlookers and witnesses. One method of helping is by using Psychological Debriefing (PD), or Critical Incident Stress Debriefing (CISD) as it is also called, and this is covered in detail in chapter 8.

Post-trauma stress is something that most will experience, but for different periods of time following the incident and in different intensity at the time or later. Some may be slightly distressed for a few hours or a few days and will then recover quite naturally and carry on with their lives. Others will suffer for longer and if the symptoms persist and intensify for more than a month they are usually identified as suffering from Post-Traumatic Stress Disorder and will need treatment. Post-Traumatic Stress Disorder is defined in the American Psychiatric Association publication *Diagnostic and Statistical Manual of Mental Disorders* (revised 1987), as 'The development of certain characteristic symptoms following a psychologically distressing event which is outside the range of normal human experience'. Again, the problem is what is and what is not 'normal'. PTSD is discussed further in chapter 8, and in *Coping with Catastrophe* by Hodgkinson and Stewart (1991).

Not everyone will suffer the symptoms of post-trauma stress, but it is important to remember: it is normal to react, but you can be normal and not react.

In other words, some will show signs of stress reactions and these can be mild or intense, short-lived or long-lasting, whilst others will seem to be unaffected in any way. The difficulty with this is that it is impossible to tell who is suffering and who is not. It is easy to look at survivors and assume that because A is screaming and shouting and running around while B is calm and cool, that A is suffering and B is not. However, A might be coping better than B because he or she is letting his or her emotions and feelings emerge. B might be bottling up everything inside and defending him- or herself against reacting. This can be rather like trying to keep the cork on a fizzing bottle of champagne. Sooner or later the champagne will explode and blow the cork high into the air. Human emotions can be the same. I might hold my feelings inside and then suddenly 'blow my top'. The problems involved are those of denial, the macho image, peer group pressure, previous experiences, expectations and social conditioning.

In spite of the evidence to the contrary, there are still some who deny that there is such a thing as post-trauma stress. One senior officer in a largely male organization said very firmly: 'My men will not suffer from stress of any kind.' Another said: 'There is no such thing as post-trauma stress except for those who have personality problems and who believe what social workers tell them.' He said this with clenched teeth, popping eyes, white knuckles and his breath coming in short pants. Yet another leader said: 'Those who believe in post-trauma stress are really trying to persuade people who are involved in disasters or trauma that they owe themselves a problem.'

All of these are very powerful denials of the existence of stress reactions. Because of this there can be deep suspicion of any approaches which attempt to deal with them. When we look at psychological debriefing we will see that the process does not suggest symptoms, but helps people to work through what they really think and feel. The focus is put very firmly on them and not on the debriefer. As an extension of this denial we need to examine the effects of the 'macho image' on people, especially in male-dominated organizations. The need to maintain a macho image can deeply affect how people respond.

It also needs to be said that some people in certain jobs and professions are dealing every day with what can be quite severe stress. Policemen, fire and rescue workers, ambulance personnel, doctors and hospital staff, clergy and those who deal with death or dead bodies, are all involved on a regular basis with incidents which could be very traumatic for others. This does not mean that they are immune to the stress, but it can mean that they have become accustomed to it and have evolved strategies for coping. Their training and experience usually takes over during the event and enables them to cope, but some might find that the strategies they use are not very effective or helpful either for them or their colleagues and families. This will be discussed later in chapter 5.

Examples of reactions
Some further examples of the effects of post traumatic stress should help us to see that the ways in which it affects people are many and varied although there are some feelings and reactions which are common to them all.

War

A young soldier on leave from Northern Ireland was staying at home with his parents. His mother became increasingly concerned because she said that he was a changed person. He was having nightmares and waking up screaming and in a sweat. He was drinking very heavily and getting drunk regularly, something he had never done before, and she would find him wandering around in a state of confusion in the middle of the night. He was irritable and sometimes couldn't control his anger or temper. She encouraged him to seek help because she believed that this condition was a direct result of what he had experienced in Northern Ireland. He had not witnessed anything terrible or traumatic, but admitted later that he was constantly terrified and afraid that he would be killed or injured. He also said that he could not show this to his friends and couldn't talk to them about it although he knew that some of them felt the same.

This man's reactions are not uncommon amongst people who are under constant stress and fear for long periods of time, but who generally manage to keep them under control until later.

A soldier who buried dead bodies in the Falklands' War said that the only way he coped was by getting drunk every night. He said that the alcohol dimmed his memories and thoughts and helped him to sleep. He also added that he was not the only one who tried to cope in this way and that it was a common reaction amongst those who had this sometimes gruesome task to perform.

He claimed that alcohol helped him to put aside what he was doing, but after the war he still had disturbing thoughts and feelings about what he had been through. As he talked about this he gradually became more and more upset until he cried about what he described as 'a few dead bodies'. He then went on to say that he did not see them as enemy, but as people who were caught up in something neither he nor they understood. His main response was one of extreme sadness and regret.

Hostages

Judy had been held as a hostage for some weeks with a group of friends. When she returned home with them she was given an opportunity to talk through her experiences and feelings. The others were content to do this, but she went into the group and, after a few minutes, walked out. A debriefer who had stayed outside in case this happened said to her that she obviously had not felt like going back into the group. She was extremely angry and upset and said that she did not need to talk about what had happened. She was all right and there was nothing wrong with her. Why should she need to talk anyway? The debriefer sat very quietly and gradually she opened up and said that she felt that she didn't belong in the group even though she knew them all intimately. She felt isolated and afraid and couldn't even bring herself to complete some simple forms. After some time she admitted that she felt that she was losing her mind and going mad and would eventually have a nervous breakdown. She started by denying that she needed to talk and then talked for almost two hours.

Judy was allowed to talk and was reassured that her reactions were normal. This was an important step in coming to terms with her feelings of anger, frustration, isolation, loneliness, listlessness and the fear that she was losing control of her mind.

Trying to avoid feelings rarely works and can cause other and longer-lasting effects. Keeping away from those who shared the experience can lead to isolation and loneliness. Paradoxically, ex-servicemen's organizations and groups formed for survivors of disasters can have the opposite effect from that intended. It also applies to other self-help groups and support organizations. A survivor of an incident said:

'I can be with those who shared the events which cause the trauma but this can isolate me from the rest of the world, including my family, who were not there. While I recognize that they do a tremendous job in supporting me and many others in and through our problems, it can mean that some of us become fixed within the group and cannot move forward. I feel that I have gone through an experience which you, the outsider, do not understand, but this can make me feel that I am alone and isolated not just by myself, but with others who belong to this exclusive club. It makes me feel special, but even more alone, even in the middle of a group of people who have shared the same or a similar experience.'

Riots

Geoff was a policeman who had been involved in a very violent and lengthy riot where many civilians were injured and some of his colleagues hospitalized. About four days later, he was in the local supermarket with his wife when he suddenly awoke to find himself sitting on the floor surrounded by a crowd of people. He felt that everything was out of his control and he just wanted to run away and hide. He was in a panic, was confused and at first didn't know where he was. As he gradually came round he found an old lady with his wife, asking if she could help him up. He started to laugh, but knew he was hiding his feelings of embarrassment, inadequacy and shame.

Such experiences can be frightening and disturbing and can occur days, weeks, months or even years later, or at times when people think that they have forgotten the incident and have learned to cope.

Accidents

In the armed services, police force, prison service and other similar organizations, there can be very strong peer-group pressure not to show emotions or feelings, especially fear.

'I remember as a national serviceman in the RAF seeing some airmen, who were in the airfield fire service, called to an aircraft which had crashed on the runway. The pilot had been burned to death in the cockpit. For weeks they would make signs and gestures when they met and curl up their bodies, hands and faces at each other and snarl. They would then laugh. This was one of the ways in which they tried to cope with what they had seen. If they made a joke about it perhaps they thought it would go away.'

Shootings

There have been cases where people have been shot dead by the police or army while carrying out armed robberies or acts of violence and terrorism. Even though the police and army have been carefully trained and the shooting was deemed necessary in order to save life, the reactions can be quite traumatic.

One man who shot an armed robber to save his own life and the lives of others reacted, 'He could have been my son.' He suffered severe shock and guilt. He was angry with himself and with the dead man, and was not sure where to place the blame and guilt. The fact that he had taken a human life was paramount: he could still see the shock, horror and surprise on the face of the man as he shot him. He was shaking with grief and couldn't cope and felt that his wife didn't understand what had happened and how he felt. He also felt a sense of isolation and that he had done something unnecessary, although he knew that it was either his life, someone else's life or the life of the robber. He had acted in a split second and made the decision to shoot when he believed that he was going to die. Facts and calm reasoning, at this stage, did not come into it. He felt dreadful, dirty and soiled.

There was nothing here of the 'Dirty Harry', 'Cops and Robbers' reaction where there is a sense that justice has been done and a feeling of satisfaction that a criminal has received 'his just deserts'. The experience is usually extremely disturbing and upsetting and there can be strong reactions following shootings even when people have not been killed. 'I am trying to save life, but I might have to take a life; in addition, my own life is at risk.'

Bank robbery

Ian was a bank clerk who was suddenly faced by a masked man with a sawn-off shotgun. The gun was thrust into his neck and face, and he was hit around the head. The man swore and cursed and threatened to kill him unless money was handed over. This ordeal only lasted a few minutes, but Ian was terrified. When the man left, Ian ran away and hid in the toilets until he felt able to face the rest of the staff and the police. A few days later he admitted to a debriefer that the worst thing for him had not been the fear of being killed but that when he was being threatened he became like an animal. 'I felt debased and dirty and would have killed him with my bare hands if I could. I felt just like an animal and almost soiled my trousers. That's how humiliated I felt. I was disgusted with myself, and still am.'

Ian was so frightened he had not been able to protect the female staff or to do anything about the gunman. He was unable to come to terms with the feeling that he had lost his own sense of value and self-worth. If he could feel able to kill, 'just like an animal', what kind of a man was he? How would he have felt if he had degraded himself further?

Divorce

It also needs to be said that post-trauma stress is not confined to disasters and accidents, but is common in situations such as divorce and separation. It is said that the three most traumatic events we can experience, in descending order, are bereavement, divorce and moving house. All of these can result in stress and post-trauma stress. When marriages break down, the result can be loss and trauma for all involved. Divorce is often tinged with the deeply disturbing feelings of guilt and failure, even when there is relief that an impossible relationship is over. The sense of relief can increase the feelings of guilt and increase the trauma.

> 'When I got divorced I lost everything. I lost my partner and what might have been a happy and satisfying relationship. I lost my house, my home and my children. Not only that, I lost my self-esteem and dignity through the whole process: the arguing and fighting, the silences and the anger, the frustration and sense of failure, the loss of self-control. I went through the screaming and shouting, the anger and bitterness, the crying and the depression. My parents don't even speak to me now. I lost my parents-in-law, and many of my friends no longer want to know me. I lost my security and feeling of belonging; I lost my status in the community. My neighbours ignore me and when I say I'm divorced, people just turn away or feel sorry for me. I also lost my job. The humiliating visits to the solicitor made me feel so dreadful and dirty; and the fighting in court for money and the children seemed so mercenary and unreal. When the decree finally came through I held it in my hand and just broke down and cried. I had failed everyone and I had failed myself. I had nothing more to lose; I had lost everything. I was afraid of what had happened and frightened of the future, and I still don't know who and what I am or where I am going. I don't think I'll ever come to terms with it.'

This kind of reaction is not unusual and is caused by the stress and trauma of the experience, especially the deeply disturbing sense of loss. This also applies to many other experiences of loss in life and this will be considered later in chapter 5.

Bereavement
Bereavement is also a traumatic experience.

> Marian was 67 when her husband, Colin, suddenly had a heart attack and dropped dead. Strangely enough, she showed no reaction at all other than to act as though nothing had happened. She didn't cry or talk about him and didn't want others to mention it. At the funeral and burial she remained calm and in control, and once the rituals were over and relatives and friends had gone, seemed to settle down into her normal routine. Three months later, her precious dog was killed by a car and Marian went to pieces, breaking down with uncontrolled grief. Her neighbours and friends who couldn't understand said, 'Fancy that! She thought more of the dog than she did of poor old Colin.' Their reaction was understandable, but they were wrong. She had bottled up her intense grief and kept it firmly under control, afraid of what would happen if she let go. She was never one to show emotion but the death of Skippy was the last straw which broke through her defences, and the flood-gates of grief were opened.

Bereavement results in the symptoms of grief and these are similar to those of post-trauma stress. This is because both grief and post-trauma stress are the result of traumatic events. Grief can be brought on by the sudden and tragic death of a child, partner or other loved one, or it can be the result of a slow and expected death following a long illness. Whether expected or not, bereavement still results in grief, although in the case of an expected death the grieving process usually begins in the form of 'anticipatory grief' before the death occurs.

The symptoms of grief, like those of post-trauma stress, can be experienced before and during the event, as well as after it. This means that the stress reactions are not just reactions after or 'post' the trauma, but can begin and be identified much earlier.

- *Before the incident.* This could be someone like a policeman or soldier preparing to face a potentially difficult or dangerous situation, or someone waiting for their own death or for the death of a loved one. It could be someone anticipating an accident, disaster or other incident which they can see or know is going to happen.

- *During the incident.* The stress reactions during the incident might be repressed or controlled and never emerge, or they might be experienced and expressed at the time.
- *After the incident.* The reactions can occur immediately afterwards or at a later stage in time, varying from a few minutes to many years.

The Iceberg Theory (Figure 1)

One way of trying to understand post trauma stress is through the Iceberg Theory.

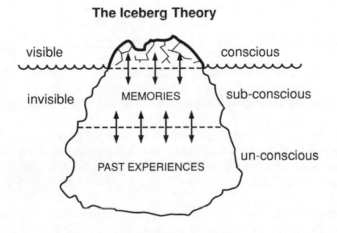

The Iceberg Theory

Every human being is rather like an iceberg floating in the sea, with only a small part visible above the water. Underneath, and hidden from view, is the major section of the iceberg. On the surface is the conscious part, that which can be seen by other icebergs as they float around in the sea. Just below the surface is the sub-conscious area in which lie our more recent memories. There are certain pieces of information which are immediately available to us and can instantly be recalled when needed: our

name, address, telephone number, the place we live in, and so on.
They are not consciously available, unless we are thinking about
them; they lie just below or on the surface.

Other bits of information are more difficult to recall or
remember – what we were doing last Wednesday, or what we had
for lunch yesterday, or the name of the person we met on the bus
recently. These can be seen as lying further under the surface in
the sub-conscious, but available when needed if we can
remember.

At a deeper level still lie our unconscious memories and
experiences. Some of these we think we have forgotten and we
would find it hard to remember them, but a name, a picture, a
sound or a smell can bring the memories flooding back.

Deeper still are experiences we have buried away and again, we
think, forgotten. The more painful these are, the deeper we have
buried them and surrounded them with a protective shell. These
can be anything from problems in childhood, concepts of self-
worth and value, what it means to be a man, woman, parent,
child, husband, father, mother and friend. Also hidden away here
are things we have done or not done, or that have been done to us
of which we are ashamed or afraid. These, and many other
distressing or disturbing experiences, are usually things we do not
wish to remember or cannot remember.

We also have good experiences buried away, but these are
usually more accessible and acceptable to our conscious minds.
We also have beliefs, expectations, hopes, prejudices, ideas and a
whole 'hidden agenda' from our character, upbringing and
environment waiting on call, some more deeply hidden than
others. Sometimes these can emerge with devastating effect.

Emma who was 26 years of age and married, was sitting
listening to some friends talking. The subject turned to child
abuse. She wasn't really listening although she was aware of
what was being said. There came a break in the conversation
and suddenly everyone sat quietly as Emma found herself
saying, 'I was abused by my stepfather when I was seven years
old.' She said that she hadn't known it before. This revelation
was almost overwhelming for her and she sought counselling
help. It transpired that she had been abused, but the memory
was so painful that she had locked it away and had forgotten
that it was there. Something in the conversation had triggered

her memory even though she said that she had talked about child abuse generally before without realizing that she was a victim. This experience was very traumatic and distressing. Counselling proved to be a very painful journey of discovering what she had buried away and why and how it had influenced her life and was causing problems in her present relationships.

Some people do not have such experiences buried away, but live with the pain of them every day. Whether buried or not, these can be very disturbing and will almost certainly influence lives in the present.

These experiences can lie deep inside our minds and the feelings and emotions associated with them are often all too ready to emerge and influence who and what we are and how we behave. A traumatic event can cause reactions which disturb the whole of the iceberg. Hidden memories and previously learned patterns of coping can be recalled and come to the surface. These may or may not be helpful in the present, in which case the feelings and emotions generated by the event can be repressed and pushed down even further into the iceberg. We deny that we are influenced or affected in any way and say that we can cope. Thus when these hidden emotions and previous experiences come to the surface they sometimes make things worse.

If I already have problems relating to attachment, loss and separation from my childhood, and I experience loss in some way or my security is threatened, these old feelings can make it more difficult for me to cope because they have been resurrected into my present life causing further insecurity and feelings of panic and pain. I may return to the same strategies I used when I was a child, and these are not likely to be helpful or positive.

In this model, post-trauma stress is not only the result of a distressing event, but also the result of our own repressed feelings and inner world, our previous experiences and the kind of help we are or are not receiving now from other people.

Summary

Post-trauma stress is the development of certain symptoms or reactions following an abnormal event. The event is abnormal in that it is life-threatening or extremely disturbing, and can be anything from a minor accident to a major disaster. This includes other incidents such as a divorce, riots, war, bereavement or any event which causes trauma and shock. This trauma is the disturbance of our normal life beliefs and turns our world upside down causing confusion, disbelief, feelings of vulnerability, a loss of meaning and purpose in life, and changes in self-image or self-esteem.

It would not be correct to assume that the symptoms are only found after the event, for they can arise earlier. The seeds of the symptoms of post-trauma stress lie not only in the nature of the event itself but also in the lives of those who experience it.

Post-trauma stress can result from any experience which, for me, is not normal; because it is not normal it can cause traumatic reactions. The experience should not be seen simply as an isolated event but rather as an ongoing situation. I bring myself, my character and personality and previous experiences, to the event and all of these, including the nature of the event, will determine how I react both at the time and later.

A man walking down a road beside a block of flats was hit on the head by a falling plant pot. This was an abnormal and unusual event and resulted in shock and trauma for the man involved. Later, he suffered from agoraphobia and the fear that the same thing might happen again if he went out into the street.

Perhaps a trivial accident, but nevertheless one which caused emotional disturbances as well as physical pain, both at the time and later.

In conclusion, many events and experiences can be seen as abnormal and result in the characteristic symptoms of post-trauma stress. We look at these symptoms in more detail in the next chapter.

Further reading

P. E. Hodgkinson and M. Stewart, *Coping with Catastrophe* (Routledge 1991)
R. Skynner and J. Cleese, *Families and How to Survive Them* (Methuen 1983)

Psychological Aspects of Disaster (The British Psychological Society 1990)

Diagnostic and Statistical Manual of Mental Disorders (American Psychiatric Association, third edition, 1987)

3
The Symptoms

In the same way that grief is the natural and normal reaction to bereavement and loss, post-trauma stress is the natural reaction following sudden or abnormal events in our lives. Stress reactions can occur not only after, but also during the event, and to some extent are dependent on the previous experiences of the people involved. If I have already experienced this particular kind of event and the stress associated with it, and have learned to cope in the past, then I will probably cope again. If the experience is new and disturbing I might have few, if any, strategies for coping and will find little from my previous life to help me at the time or later. Post-trauma stress is therefore not an isolated or unique set of symptoms which are only found once an incident has taken place. The symptoms can be there during as well as after the incident. We need to have a dynamic rather than a static view and see that the roots of the symptoms lie in the total experience of loss – from before the incident happens to the aftermath which can be weeks or years later. Therefore, in order to understand the symptoms we need to consider the previous experiences, background, character and personality of the person involved, the extent and nature of the traumatic event itself, and the quality of help and support given during and following the incident.

For example, fire and rescue workers are trained to cope with an accident. If they do suffer stress, even at a low level, their training and experience usually enable them to carry out their work efficiently. A pedestrian passing at the time of the incident might try to help, but if they have no training or previous experience to fall back on, they will probably not be able to cope. In addition, the rescue worker has the support of his or her colleagues both at the time and later, and might also have the services of a counsellor or debriefer. The pedestrian who tries to help might stagger away with no support or help from anyone and so become another victim of the accident. The person tries to cope and carry on, but has no inner or external resources from which to draw support or strength. He or she might then experience some of the symptoms of post-trauma stress and may be at more risk than the rescue worker of developing Post-Traumatic Stress

Disorder. It is impossible to say how people will suffer or who will suffer most, but through training and experience, and by providing a support system, we can reduce the risks and possible effects. What we cannot do is prevent the incident from affecting us in some way or other, no matter how little this might be. In fact the symptoms might be that we show no symptoms whatsoever! The point here is that no reaction is a reaction.

'I just got on with the job I had been trained to do. It was terrible, but I really didn't feel anything at all. Others were very upset, but not me. It was all in a day's work as far as I was concerned.'

That is how one person has responded to the incident. Whether or not they have any further reactions is difficult to say. It might be that they smoke or drink more than usual, have minor health problems or difficulties at home or work – but they might not, and seem to be the same person they have always been.

In chapter 1 it was said that being involved in a traumatic incident caused the disturbance of our basic life beliefs and resulted in a struggle to adjust, adapt and survive. This included loss of the feeling of invulnerability – 'I am not immune to disaster and I am mortal'; loss of meaning and purpose in life – 'There isn't any point'; and loss of self-image – 'I am not what I ought to be'. The resulting attempts to cope can affect every area of life and are experienced as physical, emotional, spiritual and social losses.

Physical loss

John was sitting in the front of a bus when he saw an articulated truck hurtling towards him out of control. Everything seemed to go into slow motion. His first thoughts were, 'Oh my God, this can't be happening – but it is. When will it hit us? What can I do? Am I going to die?' These thoughts flashed through his mind in the few seconds before the accident. The bus began to skid as the driver took evasive action, but there was a rending crash, the lorry collided with the coach and John's world, literally, turned upside down. He was thrown to the floor and when the bus came to a halt he slowly got to his feet to discover the bus on its side. He could hear the sounds of people screaming and moaning. He had survived, but was slightly stunned and bruised. There was a strong smell of petrol and in a panic he began to climb through a broken window, only pausing on the way to help another passenger to escape. Images planted in his mind were of broken metal and glass and bodies. He staggered away from the bus into the arms of a passing pedestrian.

John experienced a confusion of thoughts and impressions throughout this incident.

- *Before the crash*   He was sitting calmly in the bus on his way to work thinking of his family and of the proposed visit to the cinema that night. He was at peace. Then he saw the vehicle out of control coming towards him. He began to panic and felt the fear surging up inside him as he tried to prepare for what might happen. Was he going to die or be injured? Would he survive?
- *During the crash*   He felt and heard the crash as the vehicles collided. Could he escape? Was he injured? Visual images of the scene were impressed on his mind – of blood and bodies, twisted metal, broken glass and the smell of fuel. His thoughts were, 'I must get out. I must survive.'
- *After the crash*   He wondered what he had done and what he could or should have done. 'Did I do anything to help others? Was I selfish? Did I fail?' These questions were combined with feelings of guilt and shame at his own reactions of fear, panic and self-preservation.

This three-stage process was, for John, a movement from feeling secure and safe, to a rising sense of fear and impending disaster, and finally into shock, confusion, panic and guilt. This was not post-trauma stress, but a continuing experience of stress over a period of time from before the crash took place until it was over. The crash was over, but not the experience of stress.

Previously, John felt that he was reasonably in control of his life and that most things seemed to make sense. He knew that there were difficult things happening around him, but was able to push these aside and live in his relatively safe little world. A traumatic incident had disturbed this and everything became meaningless and seemingly without rhyme or reason. He looked for a way to restore the balance so that he could once again make sense of it all and, by doing so, be able to cope and carry on. All kinds of strange feelings began to churn around inside him.

He felt very strongly that part of himself had been removed. It was as though something had been torn out from his chest or stomach. Similarly, in cases of bereavement some will say they feel raw, as though their insides have been scraped out. For John it was like being battered physically by a steamroller; there was a deep sense of shock. Had he lost a leg or an arm or fingers or hand, then the sense of physical loss would have been even greater. A similar feeling of loss can also be experienced by people who go into hospital for an operation.

Physical losses are also experienced when we lose possessions and belongings: as well as losing things such as clothing, money and personal items we can lose objects like a house or the familiar sights and scenes around us that help us to feel at home and at ease. The disaster at Aberfan in October 1966, when the coal-tip slid down onto the school, not only resulted in the deaths of 116 children and 28 adults, but also changed the physical face of the village. The destruction of buildings, streets, mountains, forests and rivers can alter our perspective on the world around us – a world on which we depend and which helps us to make some kind of sense of our experiences and work out who and what we are as people. All of these are experienced as both internal and external losses. Our world is not the same, either inside or out.

Emotional loss

Bereavement

The deaths of family or friends and even of strangers, such as fellow passengers or travellers, can cause the loss we experience as grief. In the case mentioned above, John saw the bodies of other passengers lying around him and although they were strangers they added to his feelings of horror and shock, and he experienced a deep sense of grief. He had been bereaved and would need to grieve.

Loss of self-esteem and self-image

Because he had climbed out of the bus and left people behind, John believed that he had failed. His sense of failure caused a loss of self-esteem: 'I could have done more to help others.'

✻   This is a loss where John felt that he had not lived up to his idea of himself as a caring and coping human being. He also experienced the loss of his own self-image because he thought that he had failed as a man. 'I cannot be a man any more. I behaved like a selfish animal.' He had believed himself to be someone who was very much in charge of his own life and who would keep a firm grip on himself, whatever happened. This had been shattered and he now sees himself as less than the person he thought he was. 'I should have coped, but I just went to pieces.'

Loss of purpose and aim

John's life had changed; it no longer seemed to have any meaning. 'What's the point any more? Why bother to go on? What's it all about?' The ability to make any sense of his world had been thrown into confusion and he began to question the reason for living. 'How can things like this happen to me and to other people? Everything was going so well and I was minding my own business on the bus. Surely this is the result of a cruel fate? How can I go on if things can happen out of the blue over which I have no control?' John was forced to question the assumptions he had made about his life and future.

Loss of security

John is suddenly aware that he is vulnerable. He could have been killed, his wife a widow and his children left without a father. He experienced life as something that was 'breakable'. 'Nothing is certain any more. I can die. I am no longer sure of anything – my life included.' John has to try to come to terms with his own vulnerability and, perhaps, his own inevitable death. No matter how far in the future this might be, the accident seems to have brought it closer. The shock of this accident caused his whole life to be one of turmoil and confusion, and he could not see any way through. He felt angry, guilty, extremely vulnerable, isolated and victimized.

One other problem is that our past experiences, our hidden agenda, can be resurrected and cause even further confusion and disruption of our comfortable world. The shock, fear and panic we have experienced in previous events may return.

Margaret worked in a bank and was involved in an armed robbery. What made it worse was that this was the second time it had happened to her. She thought that she had learned to cope, but during and after the robbery the old feelings from the first incident, which she thought she had conquered, began to return and were almost overwhelming. She could feel the fear and see the barrel of the shotgun all over again. This made her reactions doubly difficult. On the previous occasion she had repressed the feelings, thinking they had gone away, but they returned with a vengeance and were compounded by her present experiences of fear and shock. She realized that she needed help in order to cope.

How we have learned to cope in the past, and our experiences of disaster and crises, no matter how small or trivial they were, can come hurtling to the surface. They come sliding up from the depths of our minds where we thought we had them safely locked away. If we have coped with similar crises by ignoring them and pretending they haven't happened or are not important, or that we ought to cope by being strong, then we will tend to use similar strategies in order to cope again. Some have more effective and appropriate methods of coping than others. Some will be unable to cope and others will just manage to struggle on.

Adrian was involved in a riot as an innocent bystander. He was taken to his car by a policeman. 'I just sat in my car and stared into space. I felt confused and frightened and slowly I could feel images of the blitz from the last war coming into my mind. I could hear the sirens and the explosions of the bombs. All I wanted to do was cry and run away. I sat for about half an hour and then slowly drove home. Fortunately I was able to talk this through with my wife and that helped me to calm down and cope.'

This area of emotional loss raises the problem of social and family conditioning, especially the macho image often found in men and in male-dominated organizations. If I have been brought up to deny or bury my feelings and emotions, then I will probably do the same whenever I face a crisis. (This will be discussed later.)

Spiritual loss

The feeling that our world has been turned upside down and that life is grossly unfair and unjust can destroy our deeply held beliefs, whatever they might be. It can confirm our conviction that life is a sick joke and that there is no God. Or we might discover a new faith and purpose. Either way, it can mean the loss of what we felt had made some sense of our lives and the world around us. Finding a faith through or in a crisis can be as disturbing as losing one. Some feel that conversion to a faith should be the result of dramatic and disturbing events, and so it is for some people. For others, similar experiences and events can destroy faith. However, both finding a faith and losing one involves loss, and adjusting to the changes can be disturbing and traumatic. This will be examined further when we look at bereavement and how this can affect belief. The loss of belief can cause depression, dread and a descent into meaninglessness, and the feeling that there is no reason or point in living. In John's case it meant that he was led to question the meaning of his life. If you experience an accident, disaster or bereavement, you are not usually in a fit state to be able to think things through. You cannot usually be logical or reason things out, and there are no answers to the questions people ask other than those which are generally unhelpful. To say that 'it is God's will' or 'part of some great plan' or 'just one of those unfortunate things', does not help.

Social loss

An accident or disaster can result in the loss of family and friends. We may no longer have a wife, husband, partner, parent, child or friend. Even if they are alive, whether involved in the incident or not, they might not understand what has happened to us and we can feel isolated and alone and retreat into our own little world. Also, we might not be able to cope with work and so lose our job and source of income. Work and income as well as family and friends give us a sense of purpose. The loss of any of these can result in either looking for a new identity and purpose, or retreating into apathy and inactivity. The influence of family, friends and work are important in helping us to establish our own personal and social identity. When we lose the people around us, we lose those who help us to be who and what we are.

Summary

All of these losses – physical, emotional, spiritual and social – can be experienced when a person is involved in an accident or disaster and can result in the symptoms of post-trauma stress. However, they are not separate compartments of experience, but blend into each other in the complex relationship which exists between body and mind. Each one of these influences and affects the other. The loss of a spouse or child in an accident entails physical, emotional, spiritual and social losses, all mixed up in one experience, and can cause intense feelings of grief – shock, anger and isolation, as well as loss of faith and self-worth, and a possible descent into pointlessness and depression. It may be that at the time of the incident there is little or no evidence of any stress reactions, but we cannot tell what is hidden away and repressed. Those involved in the incident may be completely unaware of their own feelings and emotions. These may or may not emerge later, and if they do they are symptoms of post-trauma stress. The reactions can be found during or soon after the traumatic incident or within a few hours or days. However, it is not quite as simple as this because the symptoms may not be present or apparent at the time and may emerge months or even years later. These symptoms can be found in a number of experiences, from bereavement or a car crash to a major disaster or where they can all be seen as reactions to trauma and loss.

Many other events in our lives result in loss and therefore in similar reactions. These losses are due to the changes we go through as we grow and develop from conception and birth to death: in childhood separation anxiety, going to school, puberty, making and breaking relationships, leaving school and home, starting work, unemployment and redundancy, falling in love, marriage, pregnancy, miscarriage and abortion, having new children in a relationship, separation and divorce, moving home, a hysterectomy, the menopause, retirement and adjusting to old age, the death of a spouse and the inevitability of one's own death. All of these, including natural and man-made disasters, entail loss, and therefore involve reactions of grief and post-trauma stress.

Characteristic reactions

While a traumatic event is taking place there will be certain emotional and physical reactions, most of which will be kept under control, but there are other specific symptoms which can occur once the incident is over. These symptoms are extensions of the experiences at the time of the event and are defined as characteristic of post-trauma stress. They can be found after the event or may emerge at a later stage and continue or intensify for some length of time when they are defined as *Post-Traumatic Stress Disorder* or *PTSD*.

In 1980, the American Psychiatric Association published the third edition of a manual entitled *Diagnostic and Statistical Manual of Mental Disorders* (revised 1987), known in short as 'DSM 3' or 'DSM III'. This gave a definition of PTSD. This was a condition which had been recognized previously in victims of concentration camps (Bruno Bettelheim, *The Informed Heart*), Vietnam veterans, and others suffering as the result of violence, disaster, accidents or war. However, the feelings, emotions and physical reactions described here can also be found in post-trauma stress. The *disorder* develops generally as a long-term reaction to the stress when the symptoms persist, intensify, and cause extreme distress and disruption of normal living.

There are three main headings under which we can place the symptoms of post-trauma stress and PTSD: *re-experiencing, avoidance, arousal.*

1. Re-experiencing

The trauma-inducing event can be experienced again hours, days, months or even years later. The feelings and emotions which were generated at the time can be felt as if they were happening *now*, in the present. They can vary from being mildly disturbing and upsetting to intense and overwhelming. The sensations and emotions felt at the time of the incident have been repressed and pushed down into the depths of the mind, but emerge and come to the surface when least expected.

(a) Triggered reactions

These feelings can be 'triggered' by sights (TV, video, media reports, news items, films, photographs, people, talking about it), and by sounds, smells, tastes and touch.

In 1984, Barry, a welfare officer in a large organization, was attending a course on bereavement. He was coping quite well until during one session the lecturer showed a film about the loss of a child. The film began with a short introduction by the producer, followed by scenes from the disaster at Aberfan in October 1966 during which 116 children and 28 adults were killed. A coal slag heap almost 800 feet high had slipped and engulfed a school and other buildings in the village of Aberfan in the Merthyr valley in South Wales. Suddenly Barry gave a shout of agony, stood up and ran from the room. He was followed by a friend from the course. Later, Barry said that he had been finding the course very helpful and was sitting calmly waiting for the film to begin. The scenes from Aberfan were quite unexpected and traumatic for him. In 1966 he had been a young miner in the next valley in South Wales, a member of the rescue team which had immediately gone to help. He said that it was as though he had been hit physically and emotions he thought had gone were resurrected in a flash. For him, the sights on the screen had brought feelings and memories flashing into the present with a force that caused him to scream with pain. This was eighteen years after the event.

Such feelings and the returning symptoms can be experienced not just weeks or months, but many years later and are brought about by some external stimulus. They can be extremely frightening and the fear of losing control or going mad is not unusual. A further fear is of not knowing when or where such triggers may be encountered; this can lead to avoidance or isolation. Some will not watch the news on television or read newspapers in case the old feelings return, whilst others will avoid friends or those who were involved with them in the incident. Even seeing a policeman or hearing an ambulance can be difficult for those who have been in an accident because it threatens to bring the past into the present.

Anniversaries, especially the first anniversary, can bring memories flooding back. This can be made worse by interest in the media or by the publication of books and articles about the event in the press or in magazines.

There may, for example, be an announcement on TV, accompanied by film of the incident. This could result in survivors experiencing feelings they thought they had managed to keep under control. On some occasions, victims will dread the advent of an anniversary and become more and more depressed or on edge as the day approaches. This can cause problems not only for them, but also for their families and friends.

(b) Spontaneous reactions

Perhaps a more disturbing way of re-experiencing the symptoms is when they are not produced by any trigger, but come 'out of the blue' and have no apparent external cause.

We can imagine what might happen if a survivor of the Zeebrugge disaster was suddenly confronted with the film *The Poseidon Adventure* on the television, a film where a passenger liner capsizes, or sees pictures from the scene of another shipping accident. We can rationalize this and say that it was the sights which caused the old feelings to be generated. It is even more disturbing if the survivor is walking down the High Street or sitting reading in bed when suddenly the feelings begin to return. In this case no external circumstances aroused the symptoms. If we see that there is an external cause, then we can probably understand it. It doesn't necessarily make the feelings any better or less disturbing, but we can say that we know what has caused them. When they suddenly spring into the present, without any trigger, this is very different. Some might feel that they are losing their minds and that they are not normal. Others manage to cope and know that whatever happens and whether there seems to be a cause or not, the feelings will go away and will not be permanent.

> Tony had been in a very severe car crash. He was a passenger in the back seat and had survived unscathed. His two friends in the front had been badly injured and all were trapped in the car until rescued by the fire service and police. The other two were unconscious, and although Tony was fully awake he was unable to move. He could smell petrol and was terrified that a fire would break out and they would be burned to death. Afterwards, both his friends recovered fully from their injuries and all went back to the local factory where they worked. One day, when he was sitting at his desk in the office, Tony suddenly began to experience a feeling of dread which seemed to start in the pit of his stomach. He could smell petrol and the same panic and fear that he had felt in the car began to return. Fortunately he had been taught some breathing exercises at

relaxation classes he had attended and he was able to control himself. Gradually the feelings began to disperse.

These experiences are sometimes referred to as '*flash-backs*', but they could equally well be called 'flash-forwards'. They can emerge gradually or suddenly from our unconscious and not only seem to take us right back to the event, but can also bring the feelings and emotions, even sights, smells and sounds associated with it, into the present.

We have buried the experiences and the feelings associated with them deep into the recesses of our unconscious and surrounded them with a protective shell. We would rather forget them, but the reality is that they do not go away. At certain times, when we are reminded of the incident, or perhaps when we are relaxing and thinking of nothing in particular, the protective shell opens and the feelings and emotions return and slide into the present. Similarly in grief after a death, there is often the belief that we will soon get over it, the feelings have gone and are buried in the past. They *are* buried, but have not gone away. They have been incorporated into our general life-map or agenda and can hover in the depths of our minds waiting the opportunity to emerge into the present. This can be a disturbing and devastating experience.

2. Avoidance

Any frightening or traumatic incident can make us very careful about being in the same situation again. If I have been in a rail accident I might be very dubious about travelling by train. A typically British response is to say, 'Get right back in there and don't let the fear conquer you', the stiff upper lip approach, which sometimes does work. If you fall off your horse or bicycle, then you might be able to get right back on again and conquer the fear. This can be a good strategy to apply to fairly minor incidents, but might not be very useful for someone involved in a more serious accident or disaster. It depends to some extent on our previous experiences, the nature of the incident, the amount and depth of fear or other feelings and emotions generated, and on our capacity to cope.

Apart from the fact that many people choose to be frightened by horror stories and films, generally we try to avoid whatever it is that makes us afraid or has scared us. Some people develop phobias about spiders, flying, heights, water, open or enclosed spaces, dogs, cats, rats, mice and just about anything else. In the same way, when we have experienced a traumatic incident, we can try to avoid anything that reminds us of the circumstances, such as places, people, pictures or other things that might bring the memories and feelings back into our minds.

As in grief, a common response to trauma is denial and this is a form of avoidance, especially amongst men. There is still the tendency in society to bring up little boys in the belief that they should not show any emotions. Girls can cry, but not men. It is common for men to say that they do not have fears of any kind, especially if they are 'real men'.

> 'If we did admit it, then our wives, friends, families and colleagues might think that we are stupid, pathetic, cowards, weak or going mad. They would also think that we were unable to cope.'

This can be particularly true for men who belong to uniformed organizations such as the armed forces, the police and prison services, and the fire and rescue service, all of which are dominated by men in positions of leadership. The macho image is difficult to stand against when you belong to an almost exclusively male club and have to keep up the image. 'You have to be strong to be a real man. There is no place for wimps or wets in this man's world.'

Showing feelings can be seen by some, especially those in authority, as revealing or displaying signs of weakness or character deficiency. Their belief is that if you are a man you will get on with the job regardless of how you feel. This is often true. A policeman can help at a terrible accident and do his job efficiently. He can bottle up his feelings at the time and afterwards may be violently sick and upset, but not in front of his colleagues. This is usually where training is important, for this can take over and help us to cope at the time even if we do have difficulties later. There is also the fear that if I admit to, or am found to be suffering from stress, my future prospects of promotion might be affected. Few people would wish this to be recorded on their confidential reports or personal documents.

Another problem faced by those in authority in these organizations can be that they interpret the possibility that some of their men might suffer from stress as a criticism of their leadership capabilities and a threat to discipline. This can cause further attempts to avoid the problems of stress by simply denying their existence.

'I am in charge here and if my men suffer from any kind of stress then it reflects on me as a leader. They are my responsibility and if they suffer stress it must be my fault. I must not have given them the training, confidence and support they need. It also means that my superiors are likely to criticize me for this and it puts me under stress and threatens my position. Also, there is the possibility of the whole thing getting out of hand. And we do not want to put ideas into people's heads. As the leader, I cannot suffer stress, therefore, there is no such thing.'

The biggest problem of avoidance is this denial of feelings. If I have been through a traumatic experience and someone asks me, 'Are you suffering from stress?', my likely reaction is to say very firmly, 'No'. I do not want other people to know how I am feeling. If I am frightened or ashamed or want to be sick I might wish to keep this secret. 'Do you need any help or counselling?' is likely to receive the same reply: 'It hasn't affected me one little bit'. I run away into a corner and cry my eyes out or remain impassive and apparently untouched. The problem is that the more I deny it and the longer it goes on, the less likely I am to acknowledge that there is anything wrong. My defences become stronger and the feelings are buried deeper in my mind. I might be able to deny my feelings to others, but can know in my own mind that I need to express how I feel. If I can do this on my own by crying or showing anger, or by talking to my wife or best friend, or someone I can trust, this might be sufficient for me to work through my feelings. If I cannot do it in any way at all, and keep everything bottled up inside, then the condition will almost certainly become worse. If the symptoms persist for more than a month and become more deep-seated and disturbing I may then suffer from Post-Traumatic Stress Disorder. However, I might not show any symptoms at all for a long time and then find that I cannot cope. Or it could be that I am unaware of the symptoms, but am ruining my marriage and causing my work to deteriorate. The result can be that others seek help either for themselves or for me. If this is the case, I will need to see a professional counsellor, therapist, psychiatrist or community psychiatric nurse. However, my defences may be so strong that they prevent me from asking for help from anyone.

Avoidance can therefore be tied in with the 'men don't cry' image of our society and the fear of losing control, either of ourselves and our own feelings or those of others, particularly those for whom we are responsible.

Avoidance can also mean keeping away from anyone or anything that reminds me of the incident, so that I become isolated within myself and feel that I am alone. On the other hand I might join a support group or club and cling to something, to someone, to a memory or to a group of people who shared the experience, and so become even more isolated and lonely.

Some develop a fatalistic view of life and believe firmly that they have little future.

> 'Life isn't really any use now and, anyway, I don't think I'll live very much longer. My marriage is in a mess and will probably break down. Also, I don't see much point in working because I might be dead soon.'

Others seem unwilling or unable to recall or remember much about the incident and some will say that they do not remember anything and refuse to talk about it.

It can also be a form of avoidance when people occupy their minds and their lives almost exclusively with the incident. Some keep a diary and live in the past or surround themselves with objects that remind them of the event. Some will involve themselves solely with memories and not stop talking about the experience. They become stuck inside their own feelings and cannot move forward. This is a form of avoidance and prevents them from living in the present or facing up to reality.

3. Arousal

Because a traumatic incident causes the nervous system to be sensitized, other symptoms can arise. It can make us 'touchy' and 'jumpy', and our reactions can be erratic and unexpected.

> 'He's not the same since he returned home. He tells me one

thing and means another and denies that he has said it in the first place and then he flies off the handle at the least thing.'

This can be very difficult for other people to live with, especially for a wife or husband, children and family or friends and colleagues. There can be an increased sensitivity to noise: the slightest sound can seem like an explosion and cause people to be startled and jump

Jamie had been involved in an accident at work where two of his friends had been killed. He survived but had been crushed under falling masonry and trapped for some hours. When he came out of hospital his wife thought he was all right, but noticed that he was very different with the children. Before the accident he would sit and watch the television in the evening while they played on the carpet and, as often happened, they would argue and fight over something. Usually, he would laugh and tell them to stop it and more often than not be found on the floor playing with them. Now he was different. The slightest noise they made would make him twitch and he would sometimes shout at them in anger. Other times he would just get up and go out into the garden and stand on his own. He was increasingly irritated by his wife and any little incident could result in a row when he would walk out of the house. He had difficulty in sleeping at night and often woke up in a sweat. At times he complained of tightness in his chest and thought that he was going to have a heart attack. He had not been violent, but showed signs of strain and constraint when they argued and she worried that he might lose his temper.

This increased sense of awareness and arousal can mean an incapacity to cope with normal events and experiences and a retreat into isolation. There can be outbursts of anger and violence between bouts of silence and a withdrawal into self.

A soldier who returned from the Falklands conflict would move from treating his wife like dirt, and abusing her verbally, to locking himself in the bedroom for days at a time. He would emerge to apologize and attempt to make it up to her, but this didn't last for long. His mood would swing from acute depression to a state of elation. His wife tried to leave him a number of times, but he would disable the car in some way in an attempt to prevent her.

There can be an increased sense of anxiety and an obsession with the fact that the incident might have resulted in your own death. You know that you are mortal and might realize that death is closer than ever before. You have seen death face to face and you are not going to put yourself into the same position again.

Another sign of this increased sense of arousal can be the desire to do things on impulse without knowing why.

Elizabeth's mother died tragically of cancer within a short period of time, and Elizabeth was with her mother when she died. The next morning, she drove into town and bought a very expensive cut-glass jug which she neither needed nor could afford. When her husband asked her why she had bought it, she said that she didn't know.

This replacement behaviour is quite common and some will spend vast sums of money on things they don't need, change their life-style or relationships and do things they have never done before. There can be the desire to move home and change jobs, to buy a new car or motor cycle and change one's image, or to get out and travel the world. Others can become dissatisfied with their relationships and look for what they see as a new and more lively partner, and marriages can break down. It is sometimes a case of, 'Off with the old and on with the new'. The effects of this can be devastating on the person concerned and on their families and friends, but they might not think that they are doing anything unusual. 'Life is short, so I might as well get as much out of it as I can. What's wrong with that?'

Re-experiencing the event, avoiding reminders, elation and arousal are typical symptoms of post-trauma stress. They may or may not be evident at the time of the incident, but can return months or years afterwards, sometimes with devastating effect.

Further reading

P. E. Hodgkinson and M. Stewart, *Coping with Catastrophe* (Routledge 1991)

Diagnostic and Statistical Manual of Mental Disorders (American Psychiatric Association, third edition, 1987)

4
Reactions

Denial

After a traumatic incident the denial of feelings can be very strong and those who use this defence will usually say that they do not need any help and that they are coping well.

Some men who had been involved in the last war, and were all taken prisoner together, came back home when the conflict was over. Most had been held in the same prison camp although some had been separated from their friends on purpose by the enemy. On their return, they were gathered together for a presentation on the possible effects of their experiences on them and their families. When it was over there were no comments or questions from them whatsoever. In fact, they made it quite clear that they were all coping and adjusting and were not suffering in any way. Their strongest defence arose when it was mentioned that they might have difficulties with sex. There was a general round of laughter and they said that none of them had any problems in this area of their lives. One member stood up immediately the presentation was over, thanked the presenters, looked at the audience and said that they were all coping quite well and would not need any help. There were grunts and nods of approval at this very positive ending!

It seems highly unlikely that a large number of men can suffer confinement, fear, and separation from their wives for a long period of time without at least one having some problems, whether sexual or not. However, what man would admit in front of his friends and in public that he had such problems? This was the result of the natural defence of denial.

Feelings

There are many feelings which can emerge.

- *Sense of pointlessness* Some will say very firmly, 'Why bother? Why go on?' 'There doesn't seem to be any reason to carry on.' Life has lost its meaning. Some will be unable to work or sustain relationships and their marriages can become very difficult or end in separation and divorce.
- *Increased anxiety and vulnerability* Being involved in an accident or disaster, or losing someone you love, can result in strong feelings of anxiety and worry. You realize that you might have died or been injured or maimed. This can cause panic and fear, but also intense sadness or, worse still, depression and a descent into apathy and inactivity.
- *Intrusive images and thoughts* People can see images of the event flashing into their minds, or these can be projected outside. They can see faces and bodies, mangled cars or train carriages, and even experience smells and sounds which remind them of the event.

  After a disaster in which many buildings were destroyed, one man said: 'I will never forget the smell of wet smouldering wood mingled with stale sweat and the smell of food cooking.'

  Thoughts can also intrude: 'Why didn't I do this or that? If I hadn't done that then this wouldn't have happened.' Maybe, perhaps, possibly, if only, might have, could have, should have, ought to have, didn't, couldn't, wouldn't, shouldn't – all these can intrude into our thoughts and we begin to question almost everything we or others did during and after the event. The images can be disturbing because sometimes they seem to bear no relation to what we have been through. Like dreams, they can be full of weird and seemingly unconnected pictures, people and scenes.

- *Nightmares and sleep-disturbances* If I have intrusive thoughts and images, and especially if I refuse to acknowledge how I really feel, then these can also be experienced in dreams and nightmares. They may come because my natural defences are down when I am asleep. They will not stay hidden and covered up because there is a need for them to emerge. These can be anything from mildly disturbing to extremely frightening, and can cause people to waken in a cold or a hot sweat, sometimes shouting or screaming and wondering where they are, even thinking that the event is happening all over again.

A soldier, after the Falklands War, said that he often had nightmares and when he did wake up in a sweat in the middle of the night, his wife would call him a 'pain in the neck' and say, 'Not again. What's wrong with you?' She didn't understand and felt that he ought to be able to cope.

There can also be disturbances in sleep patterns or inability to sleep, rest or relax, and some will go to their GP asking for sleeping tablets.

- *Shame, anger, regret, blame, guilt and bitterness* There can be feelings of shame because of real or imagined behaviour: 'I could have or should have done something to prevent it or to help. I didn't behave like a man should.'

Anger is very common and a natural reaction to trauma and loss and can be directed at anyone, self included: 'Why me?' 'Why him?' 'Why her?' An extension of anger is the desire or need to blame, and again this can be directed at anyone and everyone: God, those in authority, the doctor, the vicar, social worker, policeman, and many others – all can be blamed for what has happened. Tied in with blame is the feeling of guilt. Directing blame outside can seem very satisfying, but it is also natural to blame oneself. This causes guilt and further anxiety, sometimes in a vicious circle. I blame you so I feel guilty for blaming you, and this makes me even more guilty than before, and because I feel guilty I feel the need to blame someone so I feel more guilt – and so on. I can even blame the one who has died for being so inconsiderate as to die. This escalates the anger, blame and guilt even further. In bereavement, as in post-trauma stress, it is not uncommon to do this.

'How could he do this? We were going on our holidays next week. If he'd lived longer we would have had a better pension.'

'I hate her for dying. It should never have happened. I get so angry with her that I sometimes scream with rage.'

Blaming the person who has died can be expressed in much stronger words and expletives not printable here, but it is a natural and normal expression of anger and frustration at the loss. This can also apply when we are in an accident or disaster with someone else. The blame and anger can be directed at fellow passengers, especially those who have been killed, even if we did not know them. Bitterness is also common and there can be a deep cynicism and resentment about work, family, friends, self or life in general.

- *Survivor guilt*   Perhaps difficult to understand is the feeling of guilt at having survived. It is like a double-sided coin because I am glad that I am alive and that it wasn't me who died, but this makes me feel guilty that I am glad to have survived when others have died. Sometimes I might feel that I really wanted someone else to die and that I didn't care who died as long as it wasn't me. This intensifies the personal feelings of guilt and raises other questions.

> 'Why did I live? Why didn't I die instead? I shouldn't be here. I should be with them/him/her. A real human being (or man, leader, policeman, rescuer, father or whatever else) wouldn't wish someone else to die instead of them. This makes me feel terrible.'

This can even apply to those who were not there at the time of the incident. Some who stayed behind in this country during time of war were thankful for not being in danger, but felt guilty because they were not with their friends and comrades, especially when some were killed or injured. You can feel guilty, and even angry, that your partner or child has survived when someone else's has been killed. 'Her baby died and mine lived. Why?' 'Her husband was killed in the war and mine came home. This makes me feel terrible.'

These feelings may cause people to avoid those who suffered a loss and to feel intensely guilty. It can also result in a retreat into social isolation and loneliness. It might seem strange that it can be difficult to face life when others have suffered so much and you haven't. Words like 'fate' and 'luck' may be used and seen as directing our lives and fortunes. Some will attribute this to divine action or intervention and turn to religion for comfort and absolution.

- *Sense of isolation and loneliness*   Being involved in an accident or disaster can be terribly isolating. We have experienced something awful and feel that nobody else understands – even those who were involved in the same incident. This is true in the sense that my experiences are unique to me and even if you were with me at the time, we are different people with different life-patterns, expectations and backgrounds. Therefore each person's experiences of the same event might be similar, but they are not the same. If you have a baby who dies at three months and I lose my baby at three months, it is easy to think that we both know how the other feels. The fact is that we don't know. We share something in common, but our reactions and feelings might be different in kind or intensity. 'Nobody understands how I feel or what I went through' is a common reaction. One method of coping is by retreating into isolation or belonging to a select group who shared the experience. Belonging to such a group can also increase the sense of isolation and loneliness.

- *Fear of closed or open spaces* Some will stay at home and suffer from agoraphobia, but others will find it difficult to be confined even to their own homes. In some cases people will not want to go to their office or place of work or sit in a confined space like a car. This is especially true of incidents where people are trapped or restrained in any way. Enclosed or open spaces can cause feelings of panic and fear and the belief that the incident is happening again. They can also trigger off the feelings and emotions from the original incident and cause re-experiencing or flash-backs. This means that some will try to avoid whatever might remind them of the traumatic experience.

  Fear of crowds can also be fear of being enclosed and is a way of avoiding a situation which has caused us trauma. Groups of people can be seen as threatening or hostile. This can happen especially in busy streets, supermarkets, churches and any place where crowds or groups of people gather. It can result in further isolation and loneliness.

- *Fear of the same thing happening again* This is a natural and normal reaction, because if something has happened to me once, it can happen again, even if the possibility is fairly remote. In some contexts such fear serves a useful purpose: the child that burns its fingers will not be so likely to play with matches again. But the plane crash survivor who refuses to fly again shows a form of avoidance behaviour which can prevent a return to a normal way of life. There is nothing wrong even with this unless it becomes incapacitating or disturbing and we are unable to cope.

Behaviour

- *Inability to make decisions*   Making even simple decisions can be difficult. 'Don't ask me to fill in any forms or answer any questions because I can't do it.' 'I just don't know what to do. I can't make my mind up.' This can apply to the most seemingly trivial and unimportant tasks. When you have been through a traumatic experience the simple and ordinary things of life pale into insignificance when compared with what has been experienced. The effect can be that people who were once decisive and direct may find it hard to make decisions or know what to do and might be unable to say what they want or why they seem confused or apathetic.

- *Impulsive actions*   This has been mentioned above and applies to bereavement as well as to accidents and disasters.

- *Irritability and lack of concentration*   Some find it difficult to concentrate for any length of time and become irritable.

   > A student involved in a car crash found that he couldn't concentrate on his work either in lectures or at home. Friends said that they would find him sitting in classes just staring vacantly into space.

   This inability to concentrate can also cause more irritability and anger, which can affect all relationships – at home, at work with friends – and cause marriages to break down and relationships to end.

- *Anger and violence*   Someone who was quiet and reserved can be aggressive and unreasonable, sometimes for no apparent cause. A young man can become aggressive with his friends and a husband might turn sharply on his wife or children. There may even be violence in a marriage and this can lead to separation and divorce or to violence against children. This anger can also be directed at animals and pets. Some may even destroy personal possessions or direct their anger at things such as furniture, cars, television sets or anything else, and sometimes at objects which remind them of the event.

- *Sleep disturbances*   Dreams and nightmares as well as an inability to sleep or relax can be common. These are discussed above under 'Feelings', but they are also problems of behaviour in that they can result in pacing around during the night, shouting or screaming, sweating, panic and fear.

- *Retreat into isolation*   Someone who was gregarious and

sociable can become introvert and withdrawn. They might even cut themselves off from their family and friends. They may neglect their appearance and become scruffy, unkempt and dirty. This retreat into isolation is also discussed above under 'Feelings', but obviously has an effect upon behaviour.

Physical effects

- *Illnesses – minor and major* There can be illnesses of a non-specific nature such as headaches, stomach aches, pains or tightness in the chest and various pains in other parts of the body. Doctors might find that patients return over and over again complaining of such symptoms when there appears to be nothing physically wrong with them. The symptoms may be real or imagined, but should not be dismissed as the reactions of a hypochondriac. Doctors need to consider the possibility that the patient has been through an incident or event like an accident, disaster, loss or major change in their lives. This applies to all traumatic incidents and includes the other losses in life discussed in chapter 5, such as moving home, being made redundant, divorce, separation, getting married, being pregnant, having a baby and retirement.
- *Listlessness* Some complain of never having any energy and of being tired all the time: 'I feel washed-out and exhausted and just can't bring myself to do anything.' This might result in neglecting a home, children, partner, work or self.
- *Excitement and hyperactivity* The opposite of listlessness can occur. Some become greatly excited and hyperactive, often with no real aim in life, but may become involved in charity work and voluntary work or anything that takes their energy or activity. Others become obsessed with work or a hobby and throw themselves into these to the exclusion of most other things, including their families. There can also be an inability to rest, sleep or relax.
- *Increased or decreased physical or sexual desire* Some people become very clinging and demanding in their need for physical and sexual comfort, whilst others retreat into themselves and lose any apparent need for love or affection. This can be disastrous in a marriage or relationship especially when the behaviour is different from the norm. Either way, this can be very disturbing both for the individual concerned and for their partner and family.

'I used to be so loving and affectionate, but now I just can't seem to be bothered any more. Maybe I'm just a horrible and unloving person who doesn't or can't care about anything or anyone?'

'He's not the same person. He is so demanding and aggressive in our love-life that it just puts me off completely and then he gets annoyed and upset.'

It might even be:

'She didn't bother much before this happened, but now she just wears me out.'

- *Increased smoking or drinking*   Those who do not smoke or drink might start to do so and those who can increase their intake of nicotine or alcohol with possible effects on their health, relationships, money and work. A few might turn to drugs. If I am depressed and tired, I might believe that drugs can just give me a 'lift'. They might do this, but result in dependency and addiction with the consequent personal, social and financial problems.

Changes in values and beliefs

- *Loss of faith and purpose*   When someone has been through a traumatic incident and suffers from stress, they can change their views and beliefs dramatically: 'What's the point of marriage, having a family and a job? There isn't a reason any more. It's all a waste of time.' This can be especially true when people have lost family or friends in an accident or disaster. People and things that were important become trivial, insignificant and unnecessary. On the other hand, some become clinging and dependent and lose their sense of personal identity and self worth.
- *Problems with relationships*   Values and relationships can also be affected, and marital breakdown is a possible result of the changes post-trauma stress can bring. Spouses, if they were not involved directly in the incident, can ignore the experiences or not understand what their partner is going through. Even if they were there and also suffered stress it does not mean that they will understand or suffer in the same way. As with bereavement and grief, post-trauma stress can cause people to drift apart and break up relationships between families, relatives and friends. Some can be brought closer together by

trauma and loss, but it is common for the opposite to happen. One person can react in certain ways whilst the other shows very different responses, and this can make them drift apart. They are unlikely to share the same feelings because they will suffer in their own individual ways. A woman might look for what she sees as, 'a more exciting man than this depressed person I am living with.' The man can react by saying, 'Why should I stay with this drag?' If they are looking for more love and affection it might be difficult to get it from someone who is traumatized. As has been said above, the trauma can result in a lack of interest in sex or a renewed vigour and need for physical affection. Unless this happens to both at the same time and in the same way, there can be problems.

• *Finding or deepening faith and purpose* It has already been said that post-trauma stress can influence and affect belief, especially religious belief; some will discover a new faith, whatever that might be, whilst others will lose any faith they have. Some will be confirmed in their belief that life is without any ultimate purpose or is the result of chance or luck or even of evil forces at work in the world. Some will cling to and deepen their faith, sometimes in the face of everything that seems to go against it and others will move through their problems with dignity and calm, displaying a firm hold on reality and on their own lives.

The symptoms of post-trauma stress are similar to those of grief and loss and are typical reactions to events which are outside the normal range of our experiences. The roots of the symptoms lie in the complicated relationship which exists and takes place in the interaction between the individual concerned, their previous experiences, the nature of the incident and the support given at the time and later. In order to examine this further it is necessary to look at the nature of loss and its influence on our lives from birth to death. This is the subject of the next chapter.

Further reading

Bruno Bettelheim, *The Informed Heart* (Pelican 1988)
P. E. Hodgkinson and M. Stewart, *Coping with Catastrophe* (Routledge 1991)

Psychological Aspects of Disaster (The British Psychological Society 1990)

A. Dyregrov and J. T. Mitchell, 'Work with Traumatized Children: Psychological Effects and Coping Strategies' in *Journal of Traumatic Stress* vol. 5 (1992)

The Human Response to the Gander Military air disaster. A Summary Report (1987) (Division of Neuro-Psychiatry, Walter Reed Army Institute of Research, Washington USA)

5
Life, Loss and Trauma

The losses of living

In order to understand the nature of traumatic stress it is necessary to look at the experience of loss. Loss is one of the central experiences of all human life and is included in every aspect of existence from conception to death. From the beginning of life every human being moves from one stage of growth to another in a gradual process of change. Growing means that we move from what we have been to what we are now and, hopefully, on into the future to what we will or can be. This process involves loss because we cease to be what we were, something has gone and something new is taking its place.

We are not just 'human beings', but 'human becomings', for life is not static but dynamic; it means constant and continuing growth, change and decay. Slowly we are becoming someone new in an ever changing process which inevitably includes loss. This loss is experienced as traumatic, either in grief or in the reactions of post-trauma stress.

It might be trauma through the joy and exhilaration of winning a race, for even if this gives enjoyment and pleasure it can also cause pain and physical discomfort. It is not uncommon to feel a 'let down' or depression after a highly charged physical or emotional experience. This can be in the form of mild shock or sadness and a feeling of emptiness. We build ourselves up for it and it is gone, it is all over. A holiday is classed as a potentially highly stressful event. The preparation, waiting for transport or flights, new surroundings, different weather, language, people and food, and the many other differences and pressures can cause stress, resulting in anger, arguments, disagreements, frustration and regret. Some will return exhausted and upset about the whole experience, glad to be home, but also disappointed because the holiday is over.

It might be the trauma of having to relate to new people, a new job or a new challenge, or it can be the tragedy of bereavement, divorce or moving home, said to be the three most traumatic experiences we can have.

Whatever these changes, whether experienced as good or bad, they involve loss as we move from one state which is familiar and where we are adjusting, to one which is unfamiliar and, sometimes, deeply disturbing. The process of living involves constant growth and if we can understand some of the effects of the changes which inevitably take place, we can see how the elements of loss in them relate to the emergence of stress and traumatic reactions.

Birth and bonding

From the moment of birth, the first problem we face is that of leaving the womb and severing the contact we have with our mother through the umbilical cord. We emerge into the world naked and vulnerable relying totally on someone else for our existence. Our basic needs are for food, warmth, protection and physical contact; without these, we would die. At the moment of entering the world we experience loss – loss of the security, warmth, comfort and sustenance provided in the womb by our mothers. In the most terrible and traumatic moments of life, when people are threatened by death, when imprisoned or tortured, they may curl up into a foetal ball, perhaps in the desire to escape from pain and fear and return to the safety of the womb from which they came. As we grow and develop, our continuing experiences are of coping with change and loss. Early in life we cling to our mothers for the touch and closeness, known as 'bonding', which provides for our needs. This bonding is the essential eye-to-eye contact and skin-to-skin touch of mother and baby, which some would argue is the strongest bond of affection and love we can ever experience. This can also occur with a substitute for the physical mother such as a father, nanny, nurse, relative, foster parent or adoptive parent.

Separation and abandonment

We exist in this utter closeness to mother and, hopefully, are held and hugged, cuddled and loved, as well as fed when we are hungry. Ideally, mother supplies all our needs, but at some early stage we experience what can be a frightening and devastating event – mother is not there when we want her. We wake up and she is absent, so we scream and yell for attention. We may cry from hunger, pain or wind. The loss experienced when mother is absent can bring with it a terrifying sense of having been abandoned. Some would argue that this experience can permanently influence our whole lives through 'separation anxiety' and can produce anger, frustration and rage from deep within. We are abandoned and vulnerable. We have lost not just our mother, but part of ourselves, and our existence is threatened. This can cause feelings of internal badness and intense pain, but because these are so threatening the baby can project them onto the outside world and, in some cases, onto the mother. This projection can have a dramatic effect on the way the baby views him- or herself. Projecting bad feelings outside makes the baby feel better, but the outside world can then become a frightening and fearful place. The baby's own self-image and esteem and how he or she relates to the outside world can be damaged.

It can mean that when the baby, or the child become the adult, faces fear and trauma, their ability to adjust and cope is impaired because of their own inner conflicts. Those who have a low self-esteem or a lack of self-worth are likely to have these and other feelings intensified if they are involved in a traumatic incident where they experience the normal loss and trauma reactions of fear, threat, anger, self-blame, guilt, isolation, loneliness, loss of identity and depression.

The wider world

The next stage is when we begin to realize that there is more in the world than 'mother and me', for the two of us are seen as one person. There are other people, in an ever widening circle from father and siblings to a host of strangers peering at us, holding us and demanding our attention. Gradually we begin to explore this external world through our eyes and mouth, through touch, hearing and smell, until eventually we can crawl about and discover an even wider world around us. These are tremendous experiences of adventure and excitement that are also frightening and new, and therefore involve a sense of loss. Although we grow in confidence and strength we are moving out and away from the safety of our mother and baby oneness into the realization that not only are we separate and separated from mother, there are also others impinging on our world. Somehow, in order to exist, we have to learn to cope with them and change. This change in our lives is an experience of loss and can be deeply disturbing. We are moving from the all enclosing experience of the womb where we are totally surrounded, held and protected, to a bond with mother which is slowly being threatened as we grow and develop towards the realization that in order to be ourselves and survive we have to include others in our world.

How we cope with this loss will determine in some measure how we cope with other losses and traumas in our lives.

Teddies and toys

The move away from total dependence on mother is a traumatic and disturbing experience. In order to cope, we use different strategies to protect ourselves from too sudden a change. One of these involves the use of objects to help us through the transition from clinging closely to mother to coming to terms with the frightening outside world. These objects are referred to as 'transitional objects', the more well known ones are teddy bears and soft toys, dummies or comforters and 'comfort-cloths'. In touch and smell these remind us of, and maintain the contact with, that lost period of security and bliss when we felt we were joined with our mother. The comforter can be a thumb or finger; sometimes we see a little boy or girl, or even an older child, waddling or walking along dragging a piece of blanket or cloth, sucking its thumb, with a forefinger lying up the side of the nose. This fascinating picture is a powerful symbol of attachment and loss but shows quite clearly a child trying to integrate with and adjust to the outside world. When, as children, we do this we are reaching out, but also reaching deep inside ourselves in an effort to cope. There is a gradual change imposed upon us, from the security and safety of mother to realizing that we must move out and onwards in the process of discovery. It is in this process that we begin to find out who and what we are. Transitional objects provide the essential links between our inner world and the world around us.

Some psychologists believe that the most formative period of our lives, especially with regard to this experience of loss and its influence, is the first six months. Others argue that the period is shorter or longer than six months or is at an earlier stage, even during the time spent in the womb. If this is true, then it can be quite frightening to think that there are early experiences in life which are buried away, and perhaps of which we are unaware, which will influence how we react when we face loss through involvement in a traumatic incident or event such as a bereavement, accident or disaster.

Growing up and away

Further trauma awaits us if we have to take second place to an older or younger brother or sister and so lose our place in the family. When we go to kindergarten or school we have to learn to relate to even more people. Then there are aunts and uncles, cousins and grandparents, neighbours and family friends in an ever widening and confusing circle.

We grow from childhood through adolescence to adulthood, experiencing and carrying a whole series of losses with us. We gain in knowledge, skill and experience, but lose something of the intimacy and closeness which we have known and perhaps still desire. Meeting new people and situations means that we are forced to share ourselves and our lives further in order to grow and develop.

Growing physically can be quite a shock, especially when we suddenly feel that this is beyond our control and that we will never be the same again.

> I still remember the anger and frustration I felt at the age of nine when I realized that I could no longer fit into the motor cars on roundabouts at the fair. These were not the open-topped kinds, but the enclosed ones where you sit completely inside. I can still feel the sense of deep disappointment and anger and now see it as part of the difficult process I was going through of growing up and away from childhood and learning to accept and cope with growth and loss.

As children we experience bereavement and loss when we lose toys and teddies, but we also lose pets, relatives and friends and through these experience the pain of grief. The commonly held view that children do not grieve and should be protected from it must be wrong, for loss is already an integral part of their lives.

Going to school for the first time is a very exciting event, but means facing something new. 'You're no longer a baby. You're a big boy now'. We have moved to a new experience outside the safety of home with a host of people of all shapes and sizes, sometimes friendly and helpful, but other times hostile, threatening and aggressive.

Adolescence

In adolescence and puberty, we move in the slow and painful

transition from being a child towards adult life. We are becoming someone new and different; we increase in strength and gradually become aware of our own sexuality. Although this is normal and natural it means some degree of loss because we have moved from the relative safety of childhood to new and unfamiliar territory. The body of a young and growing man or woman also contains the mind and experiences of a child. This process of physical and emotional development involves the challenge of change and growth, but also includes the pain and trauma of loss.

There are other losses in adolescence which are also difficult to accept and work through. We may experience rejection by losing girlfriends and boyfriends, have experiences of making and breaking relationships, leaving school, going to college or university and starting work. All of these are normal, but can be difficult to cope with and may cause stress.

Adoption

For some there is the discovery that they were adopted and this can be a very painful experience: 'I am not who or what I thought I was.' There can be the search for lost parents in an attempt to rediscover the roots of our own personality and self-hood: 'Where do I come from and who am I?' This may cause problems about self-worth and value with feelings of guilt, rejection, anger and depression. 'If this can happen to me, then I must deserve it. Even if I don't deserve it, it means that somebody must have it in for me. I feel picked on, victimized and angry.'

Starting work

This is a major step in our lives for we are brought up to believe that having a job not only gives us money, but also status and dignity. It means learning to relate to new people and a different environment. It involves a new pattern of living with a great deal of change and adjustment. If I am suffering from post-trauma stress, the reactions might be so strong that I take a number of days off 'sick', or am unable to cope with work. This can affect my work or studies and eventually my career, causing further problems so that any of the effects I feel or experience are deepened and exacerbated.

Learning to love

When we fall in love we experience deeply disturbing feelings, and although this can be stimulating and exciting it indicates that we are moving from our single state to the possibility of a new relationship. This can mean a tremendous upheaval in our lives and result in the heights of joy and acceptance or the depths of sadness and rejection. Loving always includes the inevitability of losing that which we love. If I feel constantly rejected and alone, this will influence the way I react to trauma and loss.

Families and children

Being pregnant, having a miscarriage, stillbirth or abortion are all events which mean a change of state and therefore of loss and possible trauma. When children come into a family, those involved have to learn to relate in new ways and adjust. A father can feel threatened by a new baby who might be seen as a rival for the love and affection which he saw as exclusively his.

> 'Once there were just the two of us to think about, but now we are three and we have to include someone else in everything we do. It isn't the same. Things have changed and I feel angry and upset about it.'

As families grow and expand, they can include many complications and varieties, from the so called nuclear family of mother and father plus two-point-something children, to single-parent families, step-parents, step-brothers or sisters, foster parents and families, adoptive parents, children's homes and extended families. These can be immensely supportive and caring, but are also providers of stress and trauma. Patterns learned in the home and family will influence our capacity to cope with loss, trauma and stress. Our responses will be partly conditioned by the interaction between the way we have been brought up and the environment.

Divorce

Next to bereavement, divorce is said to be the most traumatic experience we can have. When a marriage ends in divorce, or a relationship breaks down, the result is loss and trauma. There are often feelings of guilt and failure, even when an impossible or destructive relationship has ended. It causes trauma for parents, children and extended families and can even be seen as a loss for the whole of society because the stability of the community seems threatened. There can be deep anger and resentment as well as feelings of rejection, failure, guilt, isolation, loneliness and depression. Again, the experience of these will affect how we respond to trauma.

> Graham's divorce came through shortly before he was involved in a car crash where he was injured. He already felt a sense of guilt, loneliness and failure and because of similar feelings resulting from the accident these were intensified and more difficult to cope with.

Retiring and growing old

Retirement from work and growing old are also major changes in the development of our lives and involve loss. We generally believe that work gives us a sense of purpose and worth and when we retire all this changes.

> 'When I retired I felt lost. One day I was somebody and the next I was nobody. I just sat around at home not knowing what to do. My job was an important part of my life and made me feel useful. I had a good income and lots of colleagues and friends in the firm. Now there's just me and my wife and she's as lost as I am. She gets annoyed at having me hanging around the house, getting under her feet and we argue a lot. I feel useless and now realize that I'm getting old. Fancy being an old-aged-pensioner! What a waste. What a loss. It makes me so angry and resentful.'

However, this feeling of being useless and redundant is not always so strong and many seem to retire gracefully. Nevertheless it is still a loss and some readjustment is necessary.

The menopause and having a hysterectomy are also experiences of change and loss and, for some, are difficult and traumatic times involving feelings of bitterness, anger, guilt, redundancy and shame.

Growing old can cause similar reactions which may be more difficult to cope with if an elderly person is involved in an incident which causes further trauma.

Death and bereavement

The death of a child, partner, parent, relative or friend is seen as the deepest loss of all. For some, one of the deepest fears we can have is the knowledge and prospect of our own death and the fear and dread that this can bring. Some take a fatalistic view and others find hope and strength through religious or other beliefs. It is said that we only truly become ourselves when we can face the fact of our own death. This can bring acceptance and peace, but many will rage against the reality of their own approaching destruction. To know that everything you are familiar with will be taken from you is perhaps the final loss that we experience, whether in the death of a partner, child or friend, or in preparation for dying and death itself. This rage against the fact of death gives a clue as to how we can cope with trauma and loss, and will be discussed when we consider bereavement and grief.

When we experience major life changes, war, accidents or disaster, at their heart can be fear – the fear of dying, of illness or injury, of hurt and rejection. Our lives have been threatened by something we do not understand; we find that we have feelings and emotions which are unfamiliar and extremely distressing. At the centre of this is the experience of loss. Something has happened to us and we have to exist with it. We have lost what we are, or thought we were, and have to try to survive.

All of these experiences in life, from conception and birth to the grave, will influence and mould the person we are at each stage in our lives. The nature versus nurture argument is relevant, for there seems little doubt that we are a combination of both as they interact with each other throughout our lives. The positive experiences will usually be helpful in enabling us to adjust to change and loss; the negative ones may inhibit our ability to cope and survive successfully. The positive side is that these bring with them the challenge to move onwards and to grow and emerge as much stronger people. However, the negative side is that this challenge also includes the possibility of stress reactions, whether sooner or later, of shock, unreality, anger, blame, depression, fear, guilt, loneliness, rejection, low self-esteem, loss of identity and isolation. When these occur after a traumatic incident, the way we deal with them will be partly conditioned by our previous life experiences. If we already have difficulty in coping with or accepting feelings and emotions such as these, they will almost certainly be compounded and made worse. This applies not only to victims and survivors, but also to helpers, rescuers, carers and the wider circle of family and friends, all of whom can be affected by the event.

Loss and trauma

The loss reactions experienced as post-trauma stress are similar to those of grief and it will help us to have a wider understanding of them if we look in more detail at bereavement and loss.

The experience of loss

Losing my car keys has almost become a habit and each time I lose them I experience the same feelings. I am annoyed that it has happened, angry at not being able to remember where I last had them, and frustrated at the sheer inconvenience caused. I cannot believe that I have lost them but I search my pockets and briefcase over and over again. I look everywhere in the office or house and hunt high and low for them. Perhaps I left them on the desk or they have slipped down the side of the chair? I even want to blame someone else. Has my wife moved them? [Is it her fault?] Have the children been playing with them? [Where can they be for they must be somewhere?] Tied in with these feelings is a sense of anxiety. I will be late for work and for my next appointment. I even feel guilty about losing them. I go through this turmoil of feelings and run around, and have other people running around, until I find them. If I don't find them, then I might sit down for a while and ask, 'What's the point of it all? Why bother?' I could scream with anger, but fall back into despair and inactivity. When I do eventually find them, I feel a great sense of relief and satisfaction and can get on with my life. On one occasion I found my keys in the deepfreeze with a book I had been reading. I was sure it must have been my wife trying to convince me that I am going mad!

This is one of life's minor inconveniences, but if I can feel such emotions over the loss of a set of keys, how much more will I feel when I lose a friend, parent, wife, husband or child, or if I am involved in an accident or disaster and face fear and death?

Throughout our lives we attach ourselves to the various things and people around us and these become necessary and familiar parts of our lives. Indeed, some of them become part of us and make us who and what we are both inside and out; they become extensions of ourselves. We only become individuals because we first learn to relate to other people and the world around us. This enables us to develop a sense of identity and self-worth. We cannot exist on our own, therefore objects as well as people become precious to us. Some would say that, at first, a baby does not see people, but objects. These objects are important and are incorporated into our world as we become emotionally and physically attached to them. The objects are not guaranteed to be with us for ever, so we are vulnerable to the pain of separation and loss which are part of the process of growth and change. In marriage it is said that 'the two become one flesh'; although we retain our separate identities, we are also part of someone else and they of us. To live and to love mean the inevitability of pain and loss. When we lose someone we love, it is called bereavement and the loss is experienced as grief. The pain of this grief cannot be cured by drugs. In fact it cannot be cured at all in the sense that some illnesses can be cured. For healing to begin we have to experience the pain and allow it to be expressed. As has already been emphasized, to cover it up or pretend it isn't there, to keep a 'stiff upper lip' or see it as something you get over, will only result in further and delayed suffering. We cannot bury the experience and the feelings associated with it and hope they will go away and not affect our lives. For the experience stays there and requires energy to keep it repressed. In our unguarded moments, or when reminded of it by something or someone, it can come to the surface with a vengeance.

The grieving process

The process of grieving can be divided into four stages, although they are not fixed or rigidly defined. Some people will go through stages 1, 2, 3 and 4 in that order, while others might move from 1 to 3 and then back to 2 and then on to stage 4. Others seem to jump about from one stage to another and the feelings and reactions from different stages are all mixed up together. However, it is convenient and useful to think of stages through which people can move. For one person, one stage might be long and drawn out, while for another it might be brief or non-existent. Sometimes the fourth stage is never reached and grieving continues at the same level without any apparent release or relief. This kind of grief is known as complicated grief and usually needs professional counselling or therapy.

If grief is allowed expression it seems to follow an identifiable pattern. There can be an initial shock, followed by a rise into anger and rage, and then a descent into the depths of depression. Gradually, if all goes well, there should be a slow ascent into healing, acceptance and peace.

Stage 1: Shock

Mrs Jones is sitting at home in the early evening expecting her husband home from work at any moment. His dinner is almost ready and she is reading the paper. Suddenly there is a knock on the door and a policeman asks if he can come in. Puzzled and a little frightened she asks what it's about. He tells her that her husband has been killed in a car accident on his way home from work.

Her first reaction will probably be of shock and she might collapse and faint or run around screaming and shouting. This shock brings a sense of numbness and emptiness as though something has suddenly been scraped out from inside. In some ways this feeling is a natural defence which enables the human mind and body to begin to cope with the unacceptable. It can continue for a long time and enable someone to go through the funeral, sort out the will, deal with insurance policies, pay all the bills, cope with the money, car and all the other tasks. Often there are sensations of coldness, weakness and unreality.

● *Unreality and denial*
Mrs Jones' immediate reaction is to say,

> 'You must have got the wrong house, it can't be my husband. I saw him this morning before he left for work. His dinner is in the oven so it can't be him. Anyway, we are going to Majorca for our holidays next week so it must be another Mr Jones.'

All of these reactions of *denial* are part of the sense of unreality which the shock can bring. Some people become annoyed and angry with the one who brings the news and refuse to accept it. 'He'll walk through the door at any moment. I can hear his car coming now.'

Others experience very strongly the presence of the one who has died. This isn't surprising, not only because of the emotional and physical attachments, but also because the home will still contain constant reminders – his clothes are in the cupboards and wardrobes, the smell of his pipe lingers, photographs are there to bring back the memories and his slippers are still beside the bed. Even the dog or cat looks for his return every day. He's there – and he isn't; this is part of the confusion that we struggle to come to terms with.

Similarly, in other traumatic incidents there can be an initial reaction of shock and disbelief and the feeling that it isn't happening. This denial can even extend to thinking that it hasn't happened at all.

● *Crying*
When they are bereaved, we expect the next-of-kin and relatives and friends to cry. This is the result of the shock and terrible feeling of sadness and loss.

> 'I just can't stop crying. I don't know what to do. I lie in bed at night and know that he's not there. I miss him so much. The tears just won't stop and I feel so stupid in front of other people. But I'll never see him again.'

Sometimes people cannot stop crying. It goes on and on and pours out for no apparent reason. You can be sitting reading or watching the TV, when suddenly a terrible feeling of sadness overwhelms you and you begin to cry. This feeling of embarrassment can be shared by others who don't know what to do or say. Helpers and carers can also share in the grief.

> Paul killed himself when his life fell apart. His wife, Joan, and the three children were away and found his body on their return. The vicar, who was a personal friend, travelled by car to see Paul's wife and on the way sat working out very carefully what he would say. He rehearsed it almost word for word. When he arrived, Joan asked him in and they went into the lounge and sat together on the sofa. He opened his mouth to speak and suddenly burst into tears. She put her arm around his shoulder to comfort him. It was also a tragic loss for him.

Crying is a natural way of relieving tension, sadness and pain and for most people is essential in the process of grieving. However, some are unable to cry and this may cause them more pain and guilt.

I should be crying but I just can't. I did love him so much but the tears won't come. I feel so empty and dried up inside that there's no room for tears.

It may be that the tears come at the funeral, in church or at the graveside, but they might not come at all. It can be months or even years later when people break down and cry.

Shock, unreality, denial and sadness are normal reactions and can also be found in those who face the trauma of an accident or disaster or other losses in the process of normal living and growing. The fact is that post-trauma stress is a natural reaction to loss and, as with bereavement, the initial response can be to erect an almost impenetrable barrier of denial in an attempt to avoid the flood of painful feelings and emotions.

Stage 2: Anger

Mrs Barber's son was killed in an accident at the factory. The funeral had been arranged and Mr Green from the factory called to pay his respects. He told her how sorry he was but found it extremely difficult to know what to say. 'I just called to say how sorry we all are about Robert . . .' And that's as far as he got. Immediately Mrs Barber shouted, 'I know it's not your fault but why did it happen to me? He's my only son. I've nobody else but his father. Look at all the other young people who waste their lives on drink and drugs. They're always in trouble. Robert never did a bad thing in his life. Why him? Why me? Anyway, why did you let him go into that place alone? He shouldn't have been there at all, the fool. He sometimes did such stupid things. And what about the doctor? He could have saved him surely if he'd got there on time. They just can't be bothered. If he had been there sooner Robert might still be alive today.'

The vicar received the same treatment as did her own doctor. The anger can suddenly burst out and be directed at anybody who happens to be there at the time, especially if they can be blamed in any way. There must be someone to blame. Other people laughing and enjoying life, or just living, can cause extreme outbursts of anger and resentment.

Such anger can be very distressing and embarrassing but, if possible, should not be bottled up inside. It should be allowed expression and accepted by others as normal, without any attempts to defend the person or organization at which the anger is directed. It may be that the anger is projected internally and is directed at self.

Anger is also common following accidents, disasters and other traumatic events. It may be directed at other victims, helpers and rescuers, bystanders and organizations, and also at self. It can be a very disturbing emotion, especially for those who believe that feeling anger is wrong and should not be expressed, even when it is felt. Some, especially men, have difficulty in coming to terms with emotions and will attempt to contain the anger and keep it under control. This might be right for rescue workers who have to get on with their job during the incident, but there should be an opportunity at a later stage for them to express what they feel.

● *Blame*

When someone close to us dies, we need to find a reason and usually want to know 'Why?' This is sometimes a practical question, but also, almost always, a question about meaning and purpose. It seems to be a natural part of the process if we can find something or someone to blame. Like anger, blame can be directed at anyone or everyone. This is sometimes the people who are seen to be responsible: the police for not preventing it, the doctor for not saving enough lives and God, who is a convenient scapegoat for just about everything else. In bereavement, blame can be directed at the person who has died, and in other traumatic incidents it can be fellow victims, even strangers, who are the focus. 'How could they go and die like that? It's ruined my life now and it's their fault. It makes me so angry. Why couldn't they have prevented it?'

This questioning can lead from anger and blame to the natural response of guilt. You can feel guilty for feeling guilty, or guilty for not feeling guilty! There can also be feelings of bitterness, regret and fear. Suddenly, and sometimes violently, your life has changed and everything seems outside your control. You are vulnerable and frail in the face of what seems to be a hostile world.

Wanting to know 'Why?' raises, what can be called ultimate questions. 'Why did it happen?', means more than wanting a practical answer. It is a cry of pain from the depths of anger and despair; no practical, trite or simple answer will suffice. Such answers can cause even deeper reactions and resentment.

In the many disasters of recent years there have been questions asked about why the incidents happened and anger and blame have been very much part of the response both from individuals and from groups set up to help survivors and relatives. The desire for recompense has been seen by some as mercenary and the result of greed, but, like anger, blame is a natural and normal response to trauma and stress. It is not simply a cry for vengeance, but a result of the desire and need for justice in what is experienced as an unjust world. Following some recent major disasters, it has seemed impossible to find answers to the questions survivors and relatives have been asking. Investigations and inquests have sometimes been inconclusive or incomplete and have not been satisfactory. This has meant that for many, anger and blame have been intensified and become extremely important issues.

● *Longing and searching*

This has been described as a burning ache deep inside for the person who has died, which almost seems to explode. It is not uncommon for someone to be found walking the streets looking for their loved one. A woman who has lost a child may look at every pram in the faint hope that she will see her baby, while a husband thinks that he sees his dead wife in the supermarket. Someone with the same build or hairstyle, or with a familiar walk, can bring the instant hope that it is them. No sooner does the hope spring up inside, than it is dashed away for we know that it cannot be true.

The desire to find and identify with the dead can be very strong when the body has not been recovered or has been destroyed through war, an explosion, air crash or fire, or when people have been drowned, lost at sea or simply disappeared. There is nothing to see and nothing to grieve over. The tragedy has happened but there is nothing in which the grief can be grounded and nowhere to focus it. This can increase the desire to find the person who has been lost.

When there is a body and it has been burnt or mutilated in some way it is often suggested that relatives should not see the body and they might be told to, 'remember him as he was'.

Catherine's son was killed in a terrible car crash and she was advised not to see the body. It was there in the coffin, but she didn't see him. Her fears and fantasies grew and although she went through the funeral and burial, she had little with which to identify. Afterwards, she said over and over again, 'I should have seen him. He was my son. I wanted to see what he looked like just one more time, even if he looked awful. I would feel better if I had only seen his little finger.' His clothes and belongings were put into the attic and nobody was allowed to touch them. Catherine believed that she had a right to see her son, but everyone prevented this and blocked every attempt she made. This made her grieving more difficult.

If Catherine had seen her son's body, it is probable that it would have helped her to come to terms with his death sooner. She constantly expected him to walk into the house and listened for the usual telephone call every Friday evening. The problem is that we think they can't be nowhere, they must be somewhere, and this can lead to a search for answers from religion. 'Surely death can't be the end?' Some will look for solace from a medium or spiritualist, while others will go over memories and try to relive the past. Photographs, videos and sound-tapes can bring back vivid memories of people which can sometimes be satisfying and helpful, but at other times distressing and disturbing.

There can be totally opposite reactions where some will destroy or get rid of everything that brings back memories while others hoard it and store it away. Often people will send things to the Salvation Army or the Oxfam shop, but still keep little things as reminders. There can never be any substitute for the person who has been lost and nothing and no one can fill the aching void which is left behind.

A similar response can be found in post-trauma stress reactions where there can be the desire to find, and identify with, other victims or to visit the graves of those killed in the incident. Some may return to the site of the disaster in the hope that it will ease the burden and provide a solution to the deep longing and ache which is felt inside.

After the Falklands War, the bodies of some servicemen killed there were brought back home at the request of relatives. The normal practice is to bury them in the country where they die. Later, relatives of those buried in the Falklands were given the opportunity to visit the graves. One mother said that as they approached the shore in a boat she expected to see her son standing there waiting to meet her. Even though she saw the grave, and this did help a little, she still expected to see her son. Often, relatives of the dead and survivors of accidents or disasters will say that a day never passes without some of the memories coming back. Longing and searching are common symptoms *both* of grief and of post trauma stress.

● *Anxiety and fear*

If my life has been threatened, and especially if I thought I was going to die, it is normal to be afraid and to feel that the same thing might happen again. Also, fear does not simply disappear once it has been experienced. It is persistent and can seem to have an existence of its own, like an evil, black cloud or monster hovering around inside and out, waiting to engulf and surround us and swallow us up. This fear and anxiety can seldom be kept at bay and is summed up in this saying by an anonymous author: 'No man can hide from his own fears, for they are part of him and they will always know where he is hiding.'

This fear and anxiety can be tied in with re-experiencing, avoidance and arousal, characteristic symptoms of post-trauma stress discussed in chapter 3. The anxiety can emerge as confusion and panic. Will it happen again? Will the feelings ever go away? Why am I so frightened and anxious? Am I ill? What am I going to do now? How will I live? Who will look after me? Will I have to sell the house and move? What about the funeral? Will I cope? How can I go on? Will I ever be normal again?

The symptoms of fear can be experienced as physical sensations. C. S. Lewis, after his wife's death, wrote in *A Grief Observed*:

'No one ever told me that grief felt so like fear . . . the same fluttering in the stomach, the same restlessness, the yawning. I kept swallowing. . . .'

If you are involved in an accident or disaster, it would be abnormal if you did not experience anxiety or fear at some level.

All of these reactions – anger, the need to blame, guilt, bitterness, regret, longing and searching, anxiety and fear – are normal and natural reactions to loss, bereavement and the trauma of accidents or disasters.

Stage 3: Depression

A descent into depression is common in grief, or following any traumatic incidents, and includes feelings of helplessness, loneliness, self-reproach, loss of identity and isolation.

The initial shock and the sense of unreality and numbness can be followed by extreme anger and, in bereavement, the clinging desire not to let go of the one who has gone. This heightened sense of activity can then descend into the depths of depression.

'What's the point? He's gone and I just can't seem to cope any more or be bothered about anything. People still come to see me but what's the use? I don't really want to see anybody. Anyway, they just don't understand how I feel. They can't, can they, unless it's happened to them? The pain seems to get worse every day. I thought I'd be feeling better by now and people told me I'd get over it in time. But it's useless trying any more. The pain and hurt just go on and on.'

The same reactions can be found in accident or disaster victims and the condition can last for many months or years. There are pictures of Queen Victoria where we see a tired and sad old lady dressed constantly in black, grieving over Albert until the day she died.

Life seems to slow down and become meaningless. Those who try to care – clergy, doctors, relatives and friends, social workers and volunteers – feel that they are facing an impenetrable barrier of depression and apathy, and those at the centre feel that it will never end.

● *Isolation and loss of self-identity and self-worth*
The experience of external loss is reflected internally through feelings of isolation and a reduced sense of self-worth or value. A disaster or accident victim, or the relative of someone killed, may feel useless, impotent and helpless.

'Before the accident I felt that I was somebody. I was good at my job and now I feel that I've lost all confidence in myself. People seem to avoid me at work and when I do speak to them they say they don't want to hear about the crash. I feel so awful and alone that I could scream, but I just retreat into myself. I suppose I'm just an embarrassment to them. People try to be kind, but what do they really know or care? It's not happened to them. I feel so lonely and isolated and don't seem to know who I am any more. I feel so useless and helpless.'

● *Loss of faith and purpose*
Following an accident in which her husband was killed, a woman who survived with her children said:

'The vicar called the other day and told me that I should be grateful that I've got the children to look after me and to remind me of John. He said that God is good, but he doesn't know what it's like for me. If God is good, why does he allow such dreadful things to happen? Life is so unfair. But why bother and what does it all matter anyway? Everything is a waste of time and of life. If there is a God, and he does things like this, then I don't want to know him.'

Some will lose faith and others find it. When someone you love has died, or when you are involved in trauma, the initial shock means that you are in no fit state to begin to think things through logically or sensibly and sweet words of comfort can be meaningless.

Some lose a sense of purpose while others throw themselves into charity work and look for some kind of satisfaction in helping other people. Some will believe that there is no purpose in life for their world has fallen apart and everything seems a complete waste of time.

● *Loneliness*
Bereavement and loss seem to carry a stigma with them.

After the accident, many people didn't know what to do or say when they met me. People don't mean to be unkind, but often they don't know what to say or do to help and the easiest course of action is either to keep away and ignore you or they never mention it. Some will cross the street or hide to avoid contact or having to speak.

There is often the fear that something will 'rub off' or that disaster and tragedy are 'catching'. This only serves to make the feeling of being alone more intense.

In bereavement, this loneliness can be further confirmed when the funeral is over and family and friends have left. For victims of accidents and disasters it can happen when they return home. The hustle and turmoil of the incident and involvement of the media all make for a high profile at the time and shortly after, but once it is over there can be a sense of abandonment and feeling that nobody cares. Relatives, neighbours and friends can be involved and give support for a short while, but they have their own lives to lead and their interest tends to wane. Their expectation is that in a short time you will be all right and and back to normal. It is easy to lose patience. Being with those who are suffering trauma and loss requires a great deal of effort and energy.

Some suggest that you must make drastic changes in your life: move house, have a holiday or go and stay with well-meaning friends or family. Sometimes these are the worst things you can do, for this only causes more change and loss. Support is important, but it is also necessary to try and retain what little sense of dignity and independence is left.

● *Physical loss*

A close relationship normally means physical closeness and sex, and when the other person dies all this is gone. It has already been said previously that trauma often means either a clinging and need for love and affection, or a complete rejection of any physical contact. Either of these reactions can cause problems.

Some people tend to lose sympathy for the bereaved as they get on with their lives. Being avoided and denied physical contact can be very hurtful and there may be a deep sense of physical and sexual deprivation.

'I can smell his presence in the house and feel that he is still here. I know he's gone, but everything around me reminds me of him. I lie in the single bed in the spare-room because our own room holds too many memories and I couldn't sleep in the double-bed without him. It feels so empty at night. I do so want to be held and loved by him, but he's not here to comfort me.'

Occasionally, some find comfort and solace with other people and sometime at a very early stage in the grief.

'Allan was 72 when his wife died in an accident and he then lived on his own for a while. Through a local club he met Judy, aged 26, and they had a mutual interest in photography. Within a short time she had moved in with him, much to the anger and frustration of his family and friends. Judy was an unwanted intrusion into their own grief and loss and some described him as a "dirty old man". They didn't understand what he was doing or why.'

Physical contact is usually very important and if you don't feel able to hug someone, just a touch on the hand or arm can be sufficient. However, some will not want to be touched or held and can seem cold and distant.

This stage of depression following trauma can last for a long time and some become trapped in their feelings of isolation and loneliness. It is as though they have descended into a pit from which they cannot escape. There is no God, nobody cares and all is without meaning or purpose.

Stage 4: Acceptance and healing

Many seem to think that grief and the reactions of post-trauma stress are relatively short-term problems that soon go away if you are determined to get on with your life and not moan or complain. Again we have the response, 'You'll soon get over it'. The belief that you will 'get over it' is partly a defence against having to be involved too deeply and a protection from thinking about what it would mean if it happened to you. Unfortunately, you do not 'get over' grief or post-trauma stress, you go into it and either stay there or go through it.

Perhaps the most difficult thing to realize is that the pain experienced contains within it the seeds of healing and renewal. Normal grief and stress reactions are not signs of an illness or sickness which needs medication or psychiatric help. Losing means pain, and the result is shock, anger and depression, and the many other complex feelings and reactions which these bring into our lives. To dismiss death or a traumatic incident as trivial or unimportant suggests either that we don't care or are defending ourselves against the unbearable pain which we know is there inside. The truth is that if we are allowed to express the pain, no matter how difficult or distressing it might be, we usually begin to cope and learn to value our lives and selves again. The pain should be 'gone through' not 'got over', for if we think that we have got over it, we will find that the terrible pain and feelings of loss remain locked away inside, eating away like a cancer and preventing us from healing and attaining peace. If the pain is experienced, we can eventually come to terms with it and learn that even at its worst it cannot destroy us: we can survive and go on. This does not mean that the pain disappears. The feelings are still inside, but we recognize them as signs that we do care about what has happened and that we are responding and reacting in a normal way to the experience. Hopefully a new sense of well-being emerges and we learn to love life once more. Yet it can be more than this, for some achieve a deeper sense of peace and acceptance and feel that they have grown in maturity, strength and confidence. Many who have survived accidents and disasters will say that when they were able to work through their experiences they emerged much more capable and self-assured. They know that they have survived and, although they didn't believe that it would ever happen, they have a new sense of their own worth and value.

This can also be true of grief. As time passes, identification with the one we have lost can become stronger than ever. In her book *Death and the Family*, Lily Pincus describes how, many years after her husband's death, she began to feel a stronger sense of his presence which increased as time went by. Her husband became more a part of her than ever before: 'Only when the lost person has been internalized and become part of the bereaved . . . is the mourning process complete.' She felt a deep sense of peace and that life was more important than ever before. This experience does not happen to everyone, but most people seem to learn to cope and carry on with their lives. They move through a host of deeply disturbing emotions and feelings and feel that their lives are still worth living. They can find new interests, new partners and friends, and new hope.

Summary

It has been stressed previously that there are losses in life other than bereavement, accidents or disasters which can also be traumatic and result in post-trauma stress. These include:

- Moving home. Long periods of separation from family.
- Going into or coming out of hospital or prison.
- Having a vasectomy, hysterectomy, losing a limb or any similar operation involving loss and change.
- Going to day or boarding school.
- Losing or leaving a job.
- Experiencing violence – robbery, war, murder, suicide, rape. Destruction of buildings and environment. Physical threat to self, family or friends.

Grieving and learning to cope with trauma is normally a long-term process and is never the same for any two people. It can divide families and couples as well as bring them together, and it can last for years. There is no easy solution except to remember that it is normal and that it takes time. In the case of bereavement, some will say that after a year they are just beginning to see their way through it, while others find that after a year the pain is worse.

However, the trauma and loss of bereavement and the experience of being involved in an accident or disaster lasts a lifetime and becomes part of our hidden agenda. It can be rather like the sea on the shore. Sometimes it surges up into our consciousness like a great wave breaking on the rocks and at other times it seems to be a memory from the past like the gentle flow of the surf over the sand.

The event, and the feelings, sensations and emotions associated with the experience, are still there buried away deep in our minds. Many months or years later, a sight, sound, smell or touch can bring the memories flooding back. The pain can still be there, but if we have been able to face the emotions and feelings and express them, we will have learned to move on in our lives. The good as well as the painful memories remain, but we have incorporated them into our life experiences and, although they may surface occasionally, we know that they are normal and cannot destroy us and that we can survive, cope and carry on with our lives.

Further reading

John Bowlby, *Attachment and Loss*, 3 vols (Penguin 1981)
John Bowlby, *Child Care and the Growth of Love* (Pelican 1953)
John Bowlby, *The Making and Breaking of Affectionate Bonds* (Tavistock 1977)
E. Erikson, *Childhood and Society* (Penguin 1965)
M. Jacobs, *The Presenting Past* (OUP 1985)
C. S. Lewis, *A Grief Observed* (Faber & Faber 1961)
Lily Pincus, *Death and the Family* (Faber & Faber 1976)
Carl Rogers, *On Becoming a Person* (Houghton Mifflin 1961)
R. Skynner & J. Cleese, *Families and How to Survive Them* (Methuen 1984)
D. W. Winnicott, *Playing and Reality* (Penguin 1974)

6
Coping

Problems in accepting trauma and loss

Certain attitudes and beliefs of the society we live in can make it more difficult for us to cope with loss, whether of bereavement, post-trauma stress or any of the other losses we experience in life. In part, these are due to the many changes which have taken place in our recent history and culture. They include denial, a common attitude to any kind of stress or loss, lack of contact with the experience of loss, reduction in social support and the use of rituals and, for many, loss of any formal religious beliefs.

Denial of the reality

It is common to deny that there is such a thing as stress. We pretend that it doesn't exist and suggest that it only affects those who are weak or lacking in moral, mental or physical strength.

If you have been brought up to believe that you should face problems with a certain toughness of body, mind and intellect, it becomes more difficult to cope with the trauma of an accident, disaster or death. 'When the going gets tough – the tough get going.' This is the good old British bulldog attitude that smiles in the face of catastrophe and crisis. Unfortunately this does not work for most of us, for it involves pushing the experiences away, deep into our minds in the hope or belief that they will not touch or affect us. The result can be that when we do experience trauma and loss, the reactions are far stronger than we might expect. The most common reaction to stress and loss seems to be to deny that they exist. Like death, accidents happen to others, not to us, and we cope by pushing them aside or inside, and ignoring them.

Lack of contact with loss and trauma

It seems to be true that people in our society are generally healthier than ever before and, on average, we live longer than our ancestors. Most people do not experience serious accidents or disasters in their lives, and death, until it comes to us, is fairly remote. Woody Allen, the American comedian, summed up this attitude when he said: 'I'm not afraid of dying, I just don't want to be there when it happens.'

Our views can easily become cold and clinical, and death and grief become more remote, partly due to the dispersal and disintegration of close family groups and ties. Children rarely see death close at hand as a normal part of life and are often discouraged from attending funerals in an attempt to shield them from the pain. Because many people move around so much and no longer live and die in the same area, old people tend not to live with or near children and their families.

There has been an increase in homes for the elderly and in sheltered accommodation. Although this might provide better care for them, it removes them from their immediate families and prevents families from having close contact with them, with old age and with death. The same can be said to some extent for the hospice movement. Although it brings many benefits such as constant professional care, relief from pain, and counselling and support for the patient and family, there are also disadvantages. It can result in a loss of contact with old age and death, and might not help us to cope with these because death becomes something to be kept in a special place rather than being a normal and natural event in life. This is far from the days when people, of whatever age, would usually die at home with their family and friends around them. The message coming across now seems to be that death, and therefore loss and the consequent feelings and emotions, are to be avoided if possible. The belief seems to be that if we shelter people from the pain, they won't feel or experience it. Pain and loss are to be seen as abnormal, as are the feelings and reactions associated with them.

This is not true of many other societies or communities where death in particular is surrounded by encouragement to grieve. Some societies even have professional mourners who can be hired for the occasion. Also, death and disaster are more common in some countries than others. Earthquakes, tornadoes, hurricanes and other natural disasters are common in some parts of the world, and some live every day with poverty, famine, disease and death as constant companions. These make the experiences of loss and trauma more common, but it does not mean that they are therefore more acceptable or less painful for those concerned. It is easy to think that because I experience disaster on a regular basis, the trauma will be easier to accept and that I will therefore cope better. This is not necessarily the case and it may be that the stresses are compounded and made worse rather than easier. When we look at the faces of starving people in the Third World we do not see the faces of people who no longer care, but of those who have almost certainly descended or retreated into numbness and a severe form of depression, helplessness and loss of purpose. These are typical symptoms of grief, loss and post-trauma stress, although the stress they experience is ongoing.

Reduced social support

When communities were closer together and smaller, it was commonplace for individuals and families suffering trauma or loss to be supported by large sections of the community. This is certainly less true since the Industrial Revolution and the move from village or small town communities to large towns, cities and conurbations, commuter districts and areas of high-rise blocks of flats. In such conditions of living, there can be little or no personal contact and for many there is less support in times of need.

> Mary had lived for eight years in a block of flats in one of the new towns on the outskirts of Liverpool, but had been brought up in the city centre and lived there until her husband retired. When her husband died she had no family to call upon other than a son who had moved to London with his family. She had no other relatives or friends. After the funeral her son returned to London and she was left to grieve alone. She lived on the eighth floor of the block, the lift was almost always broken and she did not know any of her neighbours who worked and only came home in the late evening. She was surrounded by people, but this only seemed to increase her feelings of loneliness and isolation. Within a year she had died, some said from a broken heart, but to her it seemed that nobody cared and there was nothing to live for any more.

This lack of family and community support further magnifies the stigma associated with death and loss. Our upbringing and social conditioning can tell us that these must be avoided if possible. If I have no experience of trauma and I am told to avoid it, then it will be more difficult to face and cope with. However, the fact is that loss and trauma are basic to our experiences in life. Part of the conflict is that we have our own inner experiences of losses in life and have learned various methods of coping, some of them more helpful than others, but we are told from outside, by other people, that we must be strong and not show feelings or express them. There are many mixed messages here, but they mean that our contact with grief and trauma should be minimal – to be avoided if possible.

Absence of rituals

This applies especially to death and the process of grief, but it also has significance for post-trauma stress reactions. Rituals surround the major events in our lives from birth and marriage to death, but it can be argued that in recent years there has been a tendency to reduce these. We are all very busy in our lives, especially when it comes to the pain of tragedy, and we can easily attempt to escape from any contact or involvement. The presence of rituals can be a threat to us for they remind us of the proximity and reality of death and disaster. There can be an attitude which is saying: 'Keep the rituals short for we do not want to cause further pain.'

How can you cause any more pain than already exists? If my wife has died, or I have been involved in an accident, then the pain is there, even if it is repressed and denied. Reminding me about it or talking about my wife will probably cause pain, but this is not new pain. It comes from deep within and is already there inside.

Sometimes the desire to avoid the pain is more for the benefit of those around than for those at the centre.

> At a seminar to prepare carers for coping with casualties following a disaster, someone asked whether or not the doctor should be called to give victims and survivors something to calm them down. A psychiatrist stood up and said, 'If the doctor is called, the tranquillizers should be given to those around to calm them down. You should sit with the casualty, hold their hand, give them comfort and, if appropriate encourage them to talk.'

Whose pain are we trying to avoid, the pain of the victim or our own pain?

Rituals are a necessary part of the grieving process for they enable people to focus their emotions, acknowledge the death, give permission for mourning to begin or continue, provide social, family and community support and give dignity to the dead. They also provide an opportunity not only for expressing grief, but also for showing respect and giving thanks for the lives of those who have died.

There can be little doubt that the rituals and ceremonies following the Hillsborough disaster were of inestimable benefit, not only for the survivors and relatives, but also for the carers and helpers. It was also beneficial for the nation at large, for many who watched the scenes of the disaster on the television were deeply disturbed and needed to focus their feelings and emotions and feel a sense of solidarity with those who were grieving.

Loss of belief

There appears to be a decline in church attendance and in the number of people who would definitely commit themselves to any particular beliefs. Although most people will still say that they believe in God, a survey some years ago showed that of those who go to church regularly, less than fifty per cent believe in any kind of life after death. Those who have a deep and profound faith, whether in an orthodox religion or atheism and humanism, can be helped by their beliefs to cope with grief and trauma, but it does not mean that they will not grieve.

Richard was a devout evangelical Christian who believed that everything that happened had a purpose and was part of God's greater plan. Before his wife died after being involved with him in an accident, he had been with her every day throughout the many weeks she spent in a coma in hospital. He prayed hard for her to be healed and believed in the power of prayer. When she died, he tried to remain strong and told himself that he must thank God for her life and that it was wrong to grieve for she was now with her Father. Unfortunately it didn't work. After the funeral, he was totally overwhelmed by an all-consuming grief which completely shattered his faith. He felt guilty at having survived, thought that he was partly responsible for the accident and that he had failed himself, his wife and, above all, he had failed the Church and God. He felt angry with God and descended into a state of depression where life was a waste of time and without rhyme or reason. He was going through the process of grief and post-trauma stress and didn't know it. Facing his dying wife each day had drained him physically, mentally and spiritually and trying to remain strong had only made matters worse. His Christian friends tried to help, but told him that he must pray and remember that his wife had died because it was God's will. Others said that if he had prayed harder, she might have been healed, so perhaps he lacked faith. A few more 'devout' Church members even suggested that she had died as a kind of punishment by God because of something either he or she had done wrong. It was a punishment for sin and he must look into his past life and seek forgiveness.

Little wonder that he lost his faith. It seems that he was doomed to disaster from the beginning. The faith that had been so important to him collapsed when his wife died. He believed that he would not feel any grief, and he could have done without the advice of those who claimed to be his friends.

It seems that those who do have a very strong faith and belong to a supportive community like a church or other organization, cope better than those who do not. It is said that those who survived best in concentration camps in the Second World War were those who had an inner faith and strength which came from religious or political belief. Some have said that Christians, Muslims and Communists survived better than others, and in his book, *The Informed Heart*, Bruno Bettelheim states that Jehovah's Witnesses were amongst those who coped best.

> Similar behaviour (aloofness and emotional distance) characterized another group which, according to psychoanalytic theory, would have had to be viewed as extremely neurotic or plainly delusional, and therefore apt to fall apart, as persons, under stress. I refer to Jehovah's Witnesses, who not only showed unusual heights of human dignity and moral behaviour, but seemed protected against the same camp experience that soon destroyed persons considered well integrated by my psychoanalytic friends and myself. (pp. 20–21)

Bettelheim also adds that those who survived were the ones who were able to retain their humanity amidst the terrible degradation and horror.

Those prisoners who blocked out neither heart nor reason, neither feelings nor perception, but kept informed of their inner attitudes even when they could hardly ever afford to act on them, those prisoners survived and came to understand the conditions they lived under. They also came to realize what they had not perceived before; that they still retained the last, if not the greatest of human freedoms: to choose their own attitudes in any given circumstance.

Prisoners who understood this fully, came to know that this, and only this, formed the crucial difference between retaining one's humanity (and often life itself) and accepting death as a human being. (pp. 158–59)

A firm belief and conviction can help survival, but is not an insurance policy or guarantee against suffering. The experiences of bereavement and trauma can happen to anyone and the result is loss, even if we deny it and bury it away. To believe that you will meet your loved ones again in heaven can give immense strength and comfort, but there is still the need to grieve. Jesus said that those who mourn are blessed for they will be comforted (Matthew 5.4) and perhaps he meant that in order to be blessed and comforted you need to experience the pain, for only those who do can hope to come through to healing and peace.

This is also true of any kind of trauma or loss, and to deny or try to avoid the feelings will almost certainly lead to further and deeper difficulties.

Here again we face the problem of belief when we consider the male-dominated attitudes apparent in some sections of society. It is the problem of the macho image of men which involves the belief that women should and can express emotions, but not men, at least not 'real' men; to do so is a sign of weakness or lack of character. It has already been stressed that this is a particular problem for organizations such as the armed forces, the police, the prison and fire and rescue services.

After a major air crash, male and female members of the army from a nearby camp were called in to help in the rescue and clearing up process. Some saw dead bodies and had to pick up pieces and personal belongings. Afterwards, when they gathered together to talk about their experiences, the women found it easy to talk, but the men remained silent and kept things to themselves. Few talked about it, even to their friends. Soldiers should not cry or be upset, and certainly not in front of the women!

A healthier approach would be the belief that it is all right for men to cry and show emotion, but this is not easy when you have been brought up to believe the opposite and to accept the peer-group pressure which tells you that you must be hard and tough in order to be a man. This means that if you are a man you must not cry or show emotion when you face tragedy, accidents or disaster, whether as a victim or a carer.

All of these present serious problems when we consider the way we cope with traumatic experiences and loss. Some internal and external supports have either gone or been diminished, be they social, spiritual or physical, and stress and loss reactions are seen as unnecessary. It is a healthy society that takes trauma and loss seriously and accepts as normal and natural the reactions of grief and post-trauma stress. The way in which we think about trauma and loss will determine our ability to cope with the feelings and emotions generated. It will determine the attitudes of those who suffer as victims and of those who try to help. If we are brought up to push our feelings aside and to treat sufferers as though they are ill or weak, we will be unable to face both their feelings and our own.

Coping with trauma and loss

Coping with minor stresses is a normal part of everyone's life each day. Travelling, telephone calls, letters, news, arguments, dis-appointments, anxieties and worries, problems with partners, children, neighbours, work and colleagues, are all stressful to some extent, but we usually learn to cope, even if some of them leave us frustrated, angry and upset. Coping with deeply disturbing traumatic events may cause problems which are more difficult to deal with or accept.

The ability to cope depends on a number of factors such as personality and character, previous experiences, the traumatic extent of the event and the nature of the support we are given. But it must be understood quite clearly that most people will cope most of the time and be able to carry on with their lives. It must not be imagined or believed that post-trauma stress will always damage or destroy everyone's life, for some will suffer no symptoms whatsoever and remain cool, calm and collected throughout and after the incident. However, even if it is an argument from silence, it has already been said that external reactions, or lack of them, are not necessarily indicative of the ability to cope. Nevertheless, some cope very well and claim to emerge as even stronger people with better personal relationships and marriages and a greater ability to cope in the future. The positive side of this is that involvement in a disaster can make people more aware of the importance of life and of human relationships and can help to create a strong belief in the value and purpose of life.

Human beings do have an extraordinary capacity to cope under extremely difficult conditions and events, as we have seen in the hostages released from captivity in the Middle East. Their experience was of living a life which for them was normal, then being taken hostage and enduring extreme physical and mental deprivation for years through isolation, fear, hunger, threat, torture and intimidation. Then, on their release, no matter how relieved they were, they had to come to terms with the trauma of returning to their own countries, families and friends in what must have been an alien and foreign world. Their task was, and is, to readjust to being back in a world which has developed and changed in their absence.

The same applies to service personnel returning from the many wars of this century and from the Falklands and Gulf Wars of recent years. It applies to those involved in accidents and disasters as victims or helpers, to families and friends and others in a much wider circle of support and contact. All need to know how to cope, not only with survivors and others, but also with their own feelings and reactions.

The most important things to remember about trauma and loss are:

- they are natural and normal reactions;
- they should be allowed expression;
- they involve a long-term process.

The normality of reactions
Post-trauma stress reactions, like those of grief, should be seen as completely natural and normal. They can sometimes be

overwhelming in their intensity, but even this should not necessarily be seen as abnormal. There can be problems which need professional help and counselling, especially in the case of complicated grief or Post-Traumatic Stress Disorder when the victims are trapped in a particular stage or state and are unable to work through their feelings. It also depends on the nature of the traumatic event and especially when the experience is terrifying or life-threatening. It may be connected with inappropriate or inadequate patterns of behaviour learned earlier in life as strategies for coping with problematic situations.

> Christopher had been brought up by his father to believe that 'men don't cry'. When his pet rabbit died he felt terrible, but was frightened of his father so didn't allow himself to cry. When he was eleven years old his grandmother died and he was devastated. Again, his father told him he mustn't cry and threatened to beat him if he did. Christopher's constant experience was that he belonged to a family where feelings were denied. He coped with grief and emotion by denying it and burying it inside. When he was involved with his wife in an accident, he found that he couldn't understand his wife's outbursts of emotion and was unable to cope with her nightmares and eventual depression. Gradually they drifted apart and lived separate lives. He was trapped in an emotional ice-block of denial.

Little wonder that Christopher could not begin to cope except by retreating into himself and denying the need to grieve. Another difficulty is that those who are trying to help can feel that they are being engulfed not only by the intensity of the feelings of victims and others, but by their own emotions and reactions. They retreat or become irritated and unsympathetic in an attempt to protect themselves.

Expressing feelings and emotions

There is a fairly common attitude that you soon get over grief and trauma and that within a few months at the most you will be back to normal. However, the fact is that the experience is something that has happened to you and even though you might use the defence of denial and bury it away inside, it remains part of you and will eventually find expression in one way or another. This might be through denial, silence, withdrawal and a total numbness which others can interpret as strength, or in uncontrolled outbursts of anger and violence. Especially if the feelings are repressed, it can be through various non-specific illnesses with complaints of chest pains, depression, listlessness, headaches, stomach troubles and absence from work or difficulties in relationships.

A long-term process

The experience of post-trauma stress, like that of grief, stays with us for the rest of our lives and becomes incorporated into our inner world. Even if the pain and memories have faded, they are still buried away and can emerge later as a dull ache inside or as deep feelings of regret and sadness. The symptoms can return or be expressed later and be much more disturbing.

> 'I thought that I had coped with it, but the old feelings occasionally come back and sometimes I think that I will never learn to accept them. It's very frightening, not only to experience them again, but also to know that they are still hovering inside, waiting to break out. When they do, I almost feel that they are going to engulf me.'

How long does this last? The answer is that there is no set period of time, only the knowledge that the experience will remain with us for the rest of our lives. With post-trauma stress, many people cope well at the time or within a matter of days, but some will live with the feelings for periods of varying lengths from a few weeks, to months or years. If the symptoms persist or recur for more than a month and are disturbing or disabling, Post-Traumatic Stress Disorder may be diagnosed. These reactions will depend on a number of factors already mentioned – the coping mechanisms of the individual, the nature of the event and the support given at the time and later.

People are less likely to cope if:

- the incident is particularly traumatic or life threatening;
- the individual has poor coping strategies and inner resources or a history of mental problems;
- there is lack of support – known as defusing – during the incident and shortly after;

- little or no help, counselling or debriefing is offered later.

However, it is impossible to say how anyone will cope, either at the time or later. There seem to be predisposing factors, but these may or may not be effective. Someone who appears to be coping might be suffering in silence. Another person who is crying or screaming might recover quite quickly.

In bereavement it is said that it takes on average about two years to achieve healing, but some will feel a sense of recovery earlier and some much later. A few will remain stuck with their feelings until the day they die. What is true is that if we are given support through psychological debriefing and if we can work through the feelings and emotional reactions, we will grow into a period when we feel that we are attaining some kind of peace and acceptance. Life begins to look good again, we make new relationships and move on with confidence; but the feelings have not disappeared.

> When her mother died in an accident, Katherine went through the process of grieving quite well. Four years later she was walking down the high street in the town when suddenly she began to cry. Her husband took her arm and asked what was wrong. She said that she had seen a woman who had the same hair-style and build as her mother and the memories had come flooding back. Although she had coped with her grief, the feelings were still there under the surface years later.

A clear understanding of the process of grief and the nature of post-trauma stress reactions will help all who are involved in traumatic incidents, including victims. It is necessary, not only for professional helpers such as clergy, doctors and medical staff, but also for members of the police, fire and rescue services and the armed forces. It also applies to supporting agencies such as the social services, Victim Support, Relate and other helping and counselling organizations.

Methods and strategies for coping and helping

The strategies for helping and coping suggested here are useful to everyone and anyone involved during and after a traumatic incident, from victims and rescuers to families, friends and helpers in an ever-widening circle.

The main methods of helping are similar to the ways in which people are enabled to cope with other kinds of loss. This is by encouraging them to express their feelings, work through them, and eventually discover the strength and purpose to carry on with their lives.

The following was written by Brian Keenan in an article in *The Guardian* on Friday, August 9th 1991, shortly after the release of his friend and fellow hostage John McCarthy. It reflects the words of Bruno Bettelheim quoted earlier.

Each man must find within himself the various methods to contain and control the pain and confusion within. There are no ready-made answers. It is a slow process of rediscovery, where denial or flight from the inward turmoil is the antithesis of self-healing. We go that road alone. We may be helped but we cannot be pushed or misdirected. We each have the power within us to re-humanise ourselves. We are our own self-healers.

This states quite clearly that the after-effects of a traumatic experience need to be dealt with, but that the power to heal must come from within. Others can help and give support, but it is the individual who must face the situation, discover his or her own inner resources and find the strength to go on. Denial and retreat from the feelings can only make things worse and cause further trauma. Ultimately, healing can only come from the inside and in the struggle to remain human.

The strategies and methods suggested are not the same as psychological debriefing, which will be discussed in chapter 8, although they are part of the same process of helping and debriefers should be aware of them.

We are brought up in a society which persuades us that we should deny the reality of death and hide our feelings, but the way to cope with trauma and loss is the opposite of these. There are four main tasks:

1 To help people to accept the reality of their experiences and to counteract the defence of denial.
2 To encourage them to feel the pain and to provide reassurance of the normality of their reactions. This also deals with the problem of denial.

3 To help them adjust and adapt to the changes which have taken
   place in their lives.
4 To help them redirect their emotions and their lives so that they
   can move to acceptance and healing.

Accepting the reality of the experience
Here we try to counteract the problem of denial.

Being specific about the incident
The first aim is to help people to face the fact that they have been
involved in an accident or disaster. If people have been killed or
seriously injured – strangers, relatives, friends or colleagues – this
should be talked about quite openly. If it is a death, then be
specific about the death without using flowery words or phrases.
Avoid using expressions such as 'passed away', 'deceased', 'gone
away', 'been taken from us'. Be quite direct and use the words
'death', 'dead', 'died' and 'killed'. 'I'm very sorry to hear about
Mary's death. It must be terrible for you.'

The problem is that if the experience is not talked about or the
death is denied as a fact, then soft words may prevent the other
people involved from facing the stark reality of what has
happened to them. Be precise but not brutal. Sometimes they will
try to pretend that the accident was not serious and that they are
all right, or that the person is not dead. Even years after a
traumatic incident, some will not be able to talk about it and will
attempt to keep up the pretence that all is well. In extreme cases,
some will deny that the event happened at all.

Coping with the body
● *Viewing the body*   In the case of a death in an accident or
  disaster, if it is possible, encourage relatives and survivors to
  see the body. Some will not want to do this, but should be
  gently and sensitively encouraged to do so. No matter how
  distressing the experience, it should help them to accept that
  the incident has happened and that the person is dead. They can
  see it for themselves. Also, it is an occasion when they can pay
  their respects, acknowledge the person as the one who is
  known and loved and, if it is their practice, to say some
  prayers.

  Debbie, was seven years old when she was killed playing on

a climbing frame which fell over and crushed her. Her body was taken to the local hospital and laid out in a small room. Her parents, Brian and Helen, asked the chaplain if they should see her and he suggested that it would help them if they could do so. Helen was very reluctant and didn't want to, but eventually agreed and the chaplain went with them into the room. They cried, comforted each other and stood in silence for a few minutes and then asked the chaplain to say a prayer. Shortly after the funeral, Brian and Helen had to move to another town because of Brian's work and the chaplain received a letter from them saying that they were grateful that they had seen Debbie before the funeral for they knew that if they hadn't, they would have bitterly regretted it later. It had helped them to accept her death and to grieve.

Although, in the end, their feelings and wishes should be respected, relatives should be encouraged to see the body, even if it is badly disfigured or damaged. It has been said that often the reality isn't as bad as the fantasies that can develop, either at the time or later. Even if it is as bad, or worse, it does confirm the reality of the death and help to prevent denial.

People need contact with the dead in order to help them to identify with their loved ones and accept what has happened. Viewing a body is possible when there is a body, but visiting may be discouraged because there has been a death in an aircrash, a traffic accident or other disaster when the body has been badly disfigured, mutilated or is decomposed or incomplete.

It may seem macabre to some, but many relatives say that they would like to see the body, or even part of it, no matter what condition it is in. It is important to them to have something, or literally some body, with which they can identify.

Sara's husband was killed in an air disaster and she said that she had asked to see his body, but was refused on the grounds that it was in a bad state and it would only cause her distress. She asked to see a photograph of the body and was again refused for the same reasons. Finally, she asked to see where his body had been found, but was told that this was not possible. She was extremely angry and said over and over again: 'He was my husband. I had the right to see him, or even part of him. If I could just have seen something of him it would have helped me to accept that he had died.'

- *Visiting the scene of the incident*   In the case of accidents or disasters, some may wish to visit the place where it happened. This is not absolutely necessary, but some will insist on doing so and it can sometimes be quite helpful. After the Zeebrugge disaster, some relatives of victims whose bodies had not been recovered asked to be taken on a boat trip around the *Herald of Free Enterprise*. They wanted and needed to see the place where their loved ones had been killed.

'It's not a terrible dream or figment of my imagination. This is where it all happened and this is what it did to me. I can now see that it is real.'

This will usually be very distressing, but it can help the process of grieving to continue and enable people to identify more closely with the loss and trauma that they feel.

The whole process of identifying with the incident, in whatever way, is very important for it must be seen as real so that those involved can know that their reactions are the result of a specifically distressing event. Sometimes survivors and relatives feel detached from their feelings and from the reality of what has happened; visiting the scene helps them to see that these are not made up or artificial. They do have a focus in the event and in the loss. This can come through contact with the dead or through visiting the scene of the accident or disaster. These are important rituals which help people experience their pain.

- *Talking about the experience*   Encouraging people to talk is one of the main ways of helping people to admit to and express their feelings. However, it is common for others not to mention the event in an attempt to avoid causing embarrassment or hurt, although the embarrassment is often theirs and not that of the victim. Many people who have been involved in an accident or disaster, or who have been bereaved, have a burning desire to talk about their experiences or about the person who has died. Occasionally, because of the shock and numbness, some will not wish to talk about it and they retreat into themselves, but most do talk if they are given the opportunity.

Experiencing the pain

Again, the intention is to counteract the problem of denial and of hiding away feelings and emotions. Being specific and direct about the incident, viewing the body if appropriate, visiting the scene and encouraging those involved to talk should help them to begin to accept the reality of what has happened. Although they might try to avoid it, it is presented to them as a fact over and over again and they can see it for themselves. This should help the pain to be expressed in the symptoms of post trauma stress and grief.

There must not be any attempts to avoid the feelings and people should not be told to control their emotions. 'Don't cry', and 'Don't be upset' are not helpful and can be counter-productive by causing more problems. It is also important to treat the survivor, victim, casualty or the bereaved in a way which tells them quite clearly that what they are feeling and experiencing is normal. They must not be made to feel that they are ill or sick; they may need constant reassurance that they are not stupid, weak or going mad. This reassurance can come through very strongly from others through their attitudes and in the way they are reacting and behaving. Helpers should try to convey empathy, but also that the reactions are normal.

There are certain things that will make victims aware of the situation and may help them to express their feelings and emotions.

- *The importance of rituals*   In the case of a death, viewing the body and the funeral are important events which often cause a release of emotion and feelings. They are usually in safe surroundings, with the priest or minister present and the family gathered around. This gives permission for grieving and expressing emotions. The whole process of arranging the funeral, the service in church and the burial or cremation, will usually help the pain to emerge.

  The possibility of visiting the site of the incident or disaster has already been mentioned and this can be a ritual with effects similar to those of visiting a grave or attending a funeral.

  After some accidents and disasters there have been memorial

services and ceremonies and these also are useful rituals which help people to express their grief and loss.

• *Saying the wrong things*   Helpers should encourage expression of the pain by making positive responses in what they say. Negative responses only serve to make matters worse by denying the reality of the feelings and giving the message that it is wrong to express any emotions.

> Some weeks after Jean's baby had died, she attended a formal dinner. When she arrived, a friend, trying to be helpful said, 'My word, you look absolutely stunning this evening.' Jean said afterwards, 'I could have hit him. What he didn't know was that I felt dreadful and empty inside. I didn't feel stunning.'

Comments such as this and 'Don't worry; time is a good healer' or 'I know just how you feel – the same thing happened to me' are attempts to help, but they can produce the opposite in that they stop the grief from coming out into the open and feelings get buried away even deeper inside. The positive result of these can be that they make people even more angry and upset, and if they can express this then it will help them to feel the pain. The problem is that the helper will probably be the focus of the anger and become even more defensive. 'Don't shout at me. It wasn't my fault. I only came here to help.'

Saying the wrong things can have a number of results.

• The victim, perhaps feeling vulnerable and looking for advice, accepts what is said by the helper and keeps any feelings under control by repressing them and believes that it is wrong to express emotions. 'The vicar and the doctor told me, so it must be true.'
• The victim becomes even more angry and upset and directs this at the helper. This can cause the helper to retreat.
• The victim becomes very angry, but only after the helper has left and so feels more frustrated, guilty and isolated.
• The victim silently rejects the helper and will put up the barriers whenever they call.

When the initial feelings of shock, unreality and denial combine, sometimes they prevent the pain from being felt or expressed and talking might not get through this barrier, so anyone trying to help should try to be patient and be sensitive to the reactions and feelings being expressed. However, it is important that the helper or carer is there with the survivor, for their presence alone can give comfort and help, if they refrain from saying the wrong things.

A woman whose little girl of nine had been killed in a road accident said that people often said the wrong things to her. Her advice was, 'If you can't think of anything to say, don't say anything, but just touch their arm. Someone did that to me and it meant more than a thousand words.'

It is also important that if you do say anything that you get the facts right. The difficulty is that victims, survivors and the bereaved are usually in a very sensitive state and it can be taken as a sign that you don't really care, or haven't bothered to find out, or weren't listening, if you get names, places, events and other information wrong. It is especially important to get names or relationships right for these are of prime importance. If my husband or baby is dead, then getting this wrong is an insult to their memory. However, it is fortunate that some sufferers can be extremely forgiving and compassionate. Some may be so numbed and shocked that whatever you say doesn't register anyway.

- *Saying the right things*
  (a) Say that you are sorry about whatever has happened, and, if possible, get the facts right.
  (b) Don't feel that you have to talk at all; just be there and touch an arm or hold a hand – if they will allow you to do this – but not in an intimate manner unless you know the person very well.
  (c) If you don't know what to say, say nothing.
  (d) Don't be afraid to mention the accident or disaster or talk about the one who has died.
  (e) Don't prevent them from talking about what they have experienced or are feeling and be prepared either for no response at all or a flood of words and emotions. If they do wish to talk, encourage them to do so and get them to talk about the incident or the person who is injured or dead.
  (f) Ask if there is anything you can do to help – make a cup of

tea or any telephone calls – but don't make them feel that they are incapable of doing things for themselves.

Adjusting to the changes

When someone near to us dies, we lose part of ourselves. Therefore we will need to adjust so that we can live without them and survive. This loss can be like losing half of your body or personality. 'I don't know who I am. Part of me has been torn away. He isn't there with me any more.'

In marriages, families and close relationships, as well as with friends and colleagues, we are who we are because we actively relate with them and to them. They help us to laugh and to cry, to be happy or sad. We are placed at the centre of a huge circle of relationships in which others play a part and interact with us and with each other. They determine to some extent who and what we are, depending on the nature of our relationship with them. It is rather like living on the end of a huge see-saw, with our loved ones, our life beliefs and the people and things we have become attached to, balanced at the other end. If one of those people or things suddenly falls off we crash to the ground. How strong that crash is depends on the strength of the relationship. The see-saw is unbalanced so we have to move along and adjust our position again to restore the equilibrium. This is similar to the way people cope with trauma where, hopefully, our lives are reasonably balanced and we have beliefs about ourselves and the world and a purpose in life which helps us to cope. When the basis of our lives is challenged or threatened by changes, accidents or disasters, we can become unbalanced and unable to cope. The balance needs restoring.

Two theories about why some people may manage to cope better than others are based on the ideas of *projection* and *identification*.

Projection Where individuals have developed a high sense of self-esteem throughout their lives, they tend to be able to cope on their own, and they seem to have a better chance of surviving and adjusting to trauma and loss. When someone feels that their identity is separate, this is usually because they have an inner strength and confidence which enables them to cope better than others. This seems to be true of people in marriages and relationships and may be relevant for those involved in accidents, disasters and other traumatic situations.

In bereavement and grief, the response of people in this category is usually to say, 'Something has been torn from inside me.' These people have lost part of themselves, but because they have this inner personal sense of their own identity and worth, they find it easier to adjust and cope. What they have lost has gone.

Identification There are some who can be described as 'clinging' in their relationships with others. They usually have a very low sense of self-esteem and they find it difficult to cope on their own. They have attached themselves very firmly to someone or something else and taken this inside them. They have identified this other person with themselves. They cannot exist without them and they cannot bear to be separate because their sense of worth is invested in another. This 'other' might be a person, a belief, a way of life or even a job, a house or some other object. Their view of themselves is to say, 'I cannot live without you for without you I am nothing.'

When they suffer loss these people tend to say, 'Something has died within me.' Their feeling is not that something has been taken away from them, for what has died or been lost remains dead inside them. What they have lost has not gone away. This can result in a reduction in the ability to adjust to trauma and loss of any kind.

Therefore, it seems that those who have a high sense of their own value and worth are likely to cope better with loss than those who do not.

However, if those who suffer are given the opportunity, they should be able to feel the pain of the trauma or loss and grow to accept what has happened. Some think that they will not be able to carry on with their lives but most do eventually find that they can cope, no matter how hard it is for them. As time passes, they discover that they can survive and get on with living. Knowing that you can survive can bring a feeling of relief, but it may also be tinged with guilt at having been able to cope.

Once they have begun to adjust their emotions and feelings they might discover that they can do things they have never done before. Somebody who was content to stay at home can suddenly travel the world. They can join groups and clubs when they have always been happy to stay at home. They might even find a new lease of life and become fitness fanatics, go ballroom dancing, horse riding, cycling, skiing or find some other hobby or interest. However, for some this does not happen and they experience intense loneliness and isolation for a very long time and may even hide away from others, including relatives and friends. Many, if they are given support, learn to cope on their own.

Sandra's husband was killed in an accident. When the funeral was over some friends called to see her regularly and within a few days had told her that she should be getting out and about. They belonged to a dramatic society and tried to get her to join. 'It'll do you good,' they said, 'you'll meet new people and maybe find a new interest.' When she declined their invitation, they called a number of times and tried to get her to change her mind.

They then suggested that she should go on a holiday, and when that failed they said they would take her to the keep-fit group every Thursday. This didn't work so they told her that she must find something to do outside. 'You must get out and not mope in the house. It'll only make things worse for you. You should be starting to enjoy yourself.' Eventually they gave up asking and making suggestions and told people, 'We've tried to help her, but she won't help herself.'

In fact, Sandra was grieving, and because of this was coping quite well. She did cry and felt lonely and depressed, but her daughter and son called to see her regularly to support her. However, they didn't interfere and allowed her to take things slowly. They enabled her to retain her independence and self-respect. She could cope because she had a caring and loving family around her who allowed her to mourn and wept with her. They talked about their father and often laughed at his sense of fun and spoke of the many things they had done together: the holidays and the hard times, the happy times and the many changes they had shared as a family. It took time, but almost two years later, Sandra had found herself a part-time job in a local shop and had made friends with a widower who lived a few houses away. She was surviving and coping very well.

Helping people to adjust to their trauma or loss does not mean 'jollying them along' to get out and do things and trying to force them to be happy. If they are beginning to accept what has happened and have learned that it is all right to feel the pain, even if it is sometimes almost overwhelming, they should then be moving along the road to finding out for themselves how they can adjust. Some will want to make drastic and major changes in their lives, though usually these should not be done too soon. It is generally unwise to move house shortly after an incident unless it is absolutely necessary, or to form intense new relationships or move into a marriage within a few months. This is because people's emotions and feelings might not be too stable and they can make decisions which they will regret when they have begun to recover.

Generally people need time in order to be able to move through their feelings and most, with some help, will find their own way. The way to help them is to ensure that they are beginning to accept what has happened and feel the pain. If they are doing both of these they will probably find their own ways of readjusting. If we attempt to impose our own solutions on them we might be taking away their ability to cope and only increase any feelings of inadequacy.

Redirecting emotions

When we begin to recover and feel that life has started to take on a new meaning and that we can carry on, we face the problem of what to do about our emotions, feelings and needs. It is like being left with a huge bag full of things that we need to share out but we don't know who to give them to or how to give. They seem locked up inside us. However, by the time we have moved to this stage it is likely that we have already begun to share our lives with significant people and have found some new interests. At the beginning we felt that we were isolated and alone even though there were many others around us, but gradually we have been able to talk and share our feelings. Redirecting our emotions is a gradual process whereby they slowly emerge over a long period of time and we find that the balance in our lives is beginning to be restored.

Patricia's husband Bill was killed in an accident at work when he was 50. She was 46 and their two daughters were married and had their own families in the same area. During her marriage, Pat had relied almost totally on Bill and he had done everything except the cooking and ironing. She was a 'home bird' and rarely went anywhere without Bill. At first, she was devastated and collapsed completely and her family had to do everything for her. Even nine months later she would sit in her chair and say very little although she was able to read her favourite novels. She said that she still felt that he was going to walk into the house at any time. Liz, a friend who had been at school with her and lived in the same town, heard about Bill's death so began to call regularly and they shared memories of their childhood days and how as young girls they had both met their future husbands at the same factory. Liz was also a widow and they started going out together for walks. This progressed to visits to the local pub for a drink and to the cinema.

Pat was wary of men, and felt that if she started another relationship the same thing might happen again and she wondered if another man would be like Bill. She knew inside that although she had loved Bill he had taken over her life and dominated her. She had always resented it and this had made her feel that she could not cope. She was able to talk to Liz about this and slowly she gained confidence in herself and with Liz joined a class at the local college where she studied English literature. After eighteen months she had found a man in the group who took her out frequently, and their relationship became very close. They both wanted to be sure. Pat had been supported by her family who were there giving practical help and allowing her space and time to grieve. Meeting and being with Liz helped her to go out and mix with others at a safe distance. Their talking and sharing memories enabled her to look back over her life and marriage. The interest in literature grew from her love of reading and led to meeting Jim, whom she eventually married two years later.

There may be times when we can suggest to someone that they might like to do this or that, but we must do it sensitively and carefully bearing in mind their vulnerability and need to be in control of their own lives. We must not try to take them over.

SUDDEN DEATHS

Sudden deaths are common in accidents and disasters and can cause special problems for survivors and relatives. They cause a strong sense of unreality and an even stronger feeling of guilt. There can be an increase in the need to blame somebody, in the feeling of helplessness and a deeper depression than might be expected. Survivors and relatives can ask many questions.

'If only I had seen her just once more before she died.'
'Did she know that she was dying?'
'Did she say anything before she died?'
'I feel terrible. We had a fight this morning before I left for work and we both said some awful things to each other. If only I could put this right with her.'
'I wish I had been a better husband to her. If only I could start all over again.'
'Why can't I see him just once more so that I can tell him how sorry I am and how much I love him?'
'Why do the hospital and the police have to be involved? What's it got to do with them? I don't want my baby/husband/wife/mother touched or messed with.'

Sudden deaths seem to increase and intensify the usual feelings of grief and those who help need to use different approaches.

Helping after sudden death
- There may be the need to be almost aggressive in offering help; you will certainly need to be assertive. Offer any help without asking if they want or need it. Treat it as a matter of standard practice that they should be helped. Many clergy and other helpers find that they visit without asking if they are wanted and most would say that they are never turned away. This can help to counteract the natural resistance and defences of those bereaved.
- Be specific about the accident or disaster and talk about it, even if they try to avoid it. Ensure that the loss is made clear and use the word 'dead' or 'died' as with other grief.
- Because sudden death increases agitation and the sense of vulnerability, people need to talk even more than ever and should be encouraged to do so. Making people physically comfortable is also important.
- Always make the offer of follow-up support and visit regularly, whether you are made welcome or not. Continue to visit, not just for weeks but for months and even years. Some clergy, doctors and other carers keep a register of the dates of accidents, disasters and deaths and visit on the anniversary or

send a card. A visit is better although some will say that this only serves to remind them of the event and bring back the pain. In terms of coping with pain, this can be helpful because it might unblock feelings and help to lower defences. However, there must be support for this and people should not be left high and dry.

Conclusion

The most difficult thing for anyone to understand about the reactions to trauma and loss is that the responses of whatever kind, and the pain contain within them the seeds of renewal and healing. If we are allowed and encouraged to experience this intense pain and suffering, and the many complex feelings and emotions which emerge, we can slowly come through the trauma and feel that life is worth living again. We know that life for us will never be the same, but we can adjust to new ways of living and coping.

Those involved in traumatic incidents, whether as rescuers and helpers or as survivors and their relatives or the relatives of those who are killed, should be aware of the effects of the trauma on them and on others so that they can eventually learn to cope and carry on with their lives. The methods discussed above can be used effectively with anyone suffering trauma and loss, not just from accidents and disasters, but also from other losses in life. A particular method for helping through psychological debriefing will be discussed in the final chapter of this book.

Further reading

Bruno Bettelheim, *The Informed Heart* (Pelican 1988)
Elizabeth Collick, *Through Grief* (DLT 1986)
Tony Lake, *Living with Grief* (Sheldon 1984)
C. S. Lewis, *A Grief Observed* (Faber & Faber 1961)
Colin Murray-Parkes, *Bereavement* (Pelican 1975)
Lily Pincus, *Death and the Family* (Faber & Faber 1976)
Jean Richardson, *A Death in the Family* (Lion 1982)
J. William Worden, *Grief Counselling and Grief Therapy* (Tavistock 1983)

7
Who Is Involved?

It has already been said that one of the basic problems in understanding and coping with post-trauma stress is the denial and resistance encountered in:

- society in general;
- survivors and victims;
- helpers and carers;
- those in authority.

Amongst these there are two basic core groups.

The believers These are those who believe that post-trauma stress, like other responses to trauma and loss, is a natural and normal reaction and is not necessarily a sign of weakness or personal inadequacy. They see the need for education, understanding, and awareness for everyone, especially for helpers, rescuers and carers, and for help through specialist counselling and Psychological Debriefing (or Critical Incident Stress Debriefing). We can prepare for incidents through awareness, training and co-operation between organizations and agencies, provide support at the time to help defuse the situation and give Psychological Debriefing as a standard procedure and normal response two to three days later with any follow-up necessary. As many people as possible, including survivors, rescuers and helpers, should be included in the debriefing. This is the view taken in this book.

The resisters This other group consists of those who tend to feel that post-trauma stress is the invention of psychologists and others, and that it is symptomatic of modern life and attitudes. It is the result of a drop in standards in society and a sign of a decrease in any sense of responsibility or real strength of character. Some would also take the view that because of the recent changes in society, many are less able to cope than in previous generations. For them, the answer lies in the rediscovery of old moral values and standards and in encouraging people to cope through not giving in to crisis and carrying on in spite of difficulties. There is also the tendency to deny that there are such things as depression, anxiety or stress, except for those who show signs of weakness or who lack moral purpose or strength. Sufferers are those who are weak-willed and have been brought up in a society which has gone soft.

The response of some in this group is to say such things as: 'We went through the last war and we didn't have any of this nonsense. People just got on with it and made the best of it.' However, the reality is that it is impossible to say how many people's lives, health, relationships and marriages were either damaged or destroyed because of their war experiences. There is no doubt that some returned and found it almost impossible to adjust to the changes that had taken place during their absence both in themselves and in their families. Some could not get back into their marriages or former lives and found it even more difficult to move forward. Wives and families had learned to cope on their own and found support from others, with a husband and father absent in some cases for a number of years. Perhaps one of the differences between the two world wars and those of recent times is that the whole nation was involved and there was a feeling of mutual suffering and support, whereas the Falklands and Gulf Wars did not involve everyone in the same way.

Many thousands have developed psychological, emotional and physical problems of one kind or another from all the previous wars of this century down to the Falklands and Gulf Wars of recent years. There are also the strains and stresses of living or serving in Northern Ireland and in a society where terrorism, murder, intimidation and bombings are a constant threat.

In addition, there has been a lack of understanding of the nature of trauma and loss and of the specific reactions and problems they cause. There have been great advances in our understanding of the process of grief and of responses to trauma. These show that the 'I coped and so should you' attitude is neither helpful nor realistic. It has already been argued that the macho image is very strong in our society and is presented as a defence against either showing or admitting to having feelings. This is especially true of uniformed, male-dominated organizations. The main problem lies in the attitude that you must not show any emotions; you should just get on with life without moaning or making a fuss. However, because of our increased understanding of the reactions to trauma and loss and the knowledge that expressing feelings is a necessary element in the process of recovery, such a belief and attitude is counter-productive and inevitably makes it more difficult to cope.

All people face the normal traumas and stresses of life through just being alive. These can be through something as normal as a family row or argument, or as ordinary as driving a car. Here stress is a useful reaction, for without it we would not survive the rows or journey. The right level of stress enables me to stand up for myself in a confrontation or drive safely in a world where everyone else on the road behaves like a lunatic! Stress becomes a problem when it causes distress and an inability to cope. This may come through involvement in situations which are outside my capabilities or experiences, such as new and difficult changes in life, or as the result of an accident or disaster. These are possibilities for all people. If we add to these a stressful job, then any problems, either at work or at home, can be magnified. In time of crisis we can be more at risk of experiencing stronger traumatic reactions than at other periods in our lives. Those at special risk are those whose work entails the additional stresses encountered by involvement in traumatic events.

What must be said first, before we look briefly at some of these professions, is that most do cope most of the time and are able to carry out their duties efficiently without falling apart or the experiences destroying their lives. It must not be thought that these are people who walk around with deep and unresolved problems which are blighting their lives and ruining their health and relationships. Their training and professionalism, sense of duty and pride in their work and the knowledge that they belong to a specialist group enables them to cope. However, it can be argued that these very things which help them to survive and carry on may also result in an even stronger than normal defence mechanism of denial and the repression of their thoughts and feelings. Also, all will experience stress at some level and some will suffer from post-trauma stress. Some will suffer in silence, and others will need and ask for help, but the resources to help them might not be available. The first task is to understand the pressures of their work and the special nature of their duties and then to ask what strategies they use in order to cope.

The police

By the very nature of their work in responding to the needs of the public in times of crisis, the police face many stressful areas of life. These include:

- violent family situations
- child abuse
- murder and suicides
- informing next of kin of deaths
- violence against individuals or groups
- armed robberies, muggings and fights
- hostage situations
- shootings and sieges
- rape and violence against women
- attending accidents and disasters
- attending post-mortems and inquests
- riots and strikes
- terrorist activity
- violence and physical abuse against themselves.

Like others, the police also experience the normal losses and traumas of their own lives. A policeman who is having marital or family problems or is going through a divorce or separation, may find it more difficult than usual to cope with his work and colleagues may be aware, because of his behaviour, that all is not well.

Also, how do police officers, like any other helpers, attend a particularly traumatic incident where they see the mangled bodies of men, women and children and the reactions of survivors, and then go home and relax with their families? Most do cope, but in what ways and how does it affect them?

After the Lockerbie air disaster, the police and the army, amongst other services, were called in to help. Most of the soldiers were from the same regiment, knew each other well, had trained with each other, had their own chaplains with them and had a strong sense of solidarity. Many of the police were not local, but had been brought in from outside and then returned home each day. The soldiers worked together, slept together, ate together and stayed together, and so were able to talk and share their experiences and feelings late into the night. The police travelled home either on coaches or in their own transport and there was little opportunity for many of them to talk and share what they saw and felt.

Because of these differences, some believe that the soldiers were better able to cope with the traumas they faced each day and there have been reports in the press of police officers who were involved at Lockerbie suffering from post-trauma stress with increased rates of absenteeism, poor health and problems in relationships. It would be interesting to know the reactions, experiences and opinions of their spouses and families. What seems to be true is that a cohesive and closely-knit group of people are more likely to cope in a traumatic incident than individuals who do not know each other, have not worked together before and do not have much opportunity to talk to each other.

However, it could be argued that because of the differences, the soldiers were better able to hide and control their true feelings and only talked about things on the surface. It could be that the cohesiveness of a group enables the members to cope better at the time, but that some may develop problems later which only emerge occasionally in symptoms with an unacknowledged cause or source. Did they show their real feelings and express them, and therefore not exhibit many or any of the symptoms of post-trauma stress, or were they more able to repress them? The report on coping strategies discussed later, written by Dyregrov and Mitchell following a bus crash in Norway in which many children were killed, is relevant. What must be kept in mind is that because people have better coping strategies during the incident it does not mean that they will not have any reactions later. Neither does it mean that they will.

Training and co-operation are also important and there is little doubt that the emergency services, including the police, who helped after the East Midlands air crash near Kegworth on the M1, were able to cope better because they had trained together on a simulated disaster exercise not long before the accident.

The police have their own support services through their welfare officers and some forces already have, or are looking very seriously at having, professionally trained counsellors skilled in psychological debriefing to help police personnel not only after accidents, disasters and major emergencies, but also following other traumatic incidents.

There is also the support, usual in all uniformed organizations, of the chain of command, and those in positions of authority normally feel a sense of responsibility for their men and will look after and be interested in their welfare. However, it is not sufficient for senior officers to say that after a difficult incident they always have their men and women in to see them to check if they are all right and to let them talk. This does show that they care, but it needs to be done in a more professional and structured manner as is provided through proper Psychological Debriefing. Police personnel may not wish to tell their superiors how they do feel or what problems they are having, possibly because of their own macho-style self-image, their anxieties about the opinions of their colleagues and the effect on their personal reports and, therefore, their careers. In any case, the typical post-trauma stress reactions and natural defence mechanisms of denial will be operating, even if those involved have few concerns about their images or future. Properly trained support is essential.

Fire and rescue services

Like the police, the fire and rescue services are involved in accidents and disasters and they may have to extract victims and survivors from buildings or vehicles. They may even be called upon to rescue a child or a cat from a tree or someone with their head trapped in railings. On some occasions they will be in situations of extreme danger and their lives will be at risk. Although they are highly trained for such emergencies, it still means that they experience life-threatening incidents and, therefore, stress and trauma. They might have to put their lives in danger, see survivors and the dead sometimes in a badly burned or mutilated condition, and they will be expected to cope.

At a conference on coping with trauma held in Colchester in 1989 attended by members of the emergency services from a number of counties, some fire and rescue officers said that in their area they believed that they were able to cope and did not need specialist counselling or help. They felt that because they worked on 'watch' in teams, they were able to share their thoughts, feelings and experiences when they returned to the station. This, they said, meant that they did not have any great problems and were helped to cope. However, what they were talking about was 'defusing' and not 'debriefing'.

We can ask the same question as before: Did they talk at a deep level and really say how they felt, or was the talking a way of defending their true feelings and emotions, even if it did help them to cope? Methods for coping at the time and shortly after are not the same as dealing with the feelings and emotions generated. They may simply result in burying them deeper inside.

Also, if women are present as part of the team, will this cause the men to be more macho than normal because they feel that they have to cope in front of women, or will the reactions of the women, who may be better able to show their feelings, help them to feel that they can safely talk more openly? It might even be that the women, instead of being able to bring out their feelings and express their emotions, try to be like the men and show that they also can be strong.

Men	'Women are present, so I must be strong and not show any signs of weakness.'
	'The women are being emotional so I must remain strong for them and be a shoulder to cry on.'
	'The women are crying and upset, so that gives me permission to do the same.'
Women	'I'm a woman so the men won't mind if I cry.'
	'I'm a woman, but will show these men that I'm not weak. I won't cry or get upset.'

The fire and rescue services also have support through welfare officers. Some counties do have personnel trained in counselling and Psychological Debriefing and there are some who do have debriefing as standard procedure. This must be for everyone and not just for those who may seem to be suffering. Part of the problem is that if they are given an opportunity to choose, many will probably decline the invitation and these may be the very ones who need help most. Having debriefing for all as normal, standard procedure removes the need to ask and can counteract the defences of denial.

Ambulance crews

Ambulance crews also attend traumatic situations, from accidents, disasters, shootings and bombings, to heart attacks, attempted or successful suicides or murders, medical crises, deaths, pregnancies, births, miscarriages, abortions and a variety of incidents where there is violence, abuse or injury. They would normally be involved in most incidents where the police and fire and rescue services are present.

Like the other professional services they are highly trained and usually work in pairs in one vehicle or in teams with men and women working together. Their lives may occasionally be at risk and they will see suffering and death at close quarters. They have to be on stand-by in case of call-out and therefore work in a situation where they will experience stress and trauma. Sometimes their work is extremely frustrating especially where initially they may have to remain at some distance from an incident to assess needs or where they are unable to save life. This places them under further strain.

Their needs are exactly the same as those of the police and fire and rescue services. There should be training in awareness of the effects of post-trauma stress, support and after-care for them following involvement in difficult situations. After some incidents they will need counselling and Psychological Debriefing.

The armed services

Members of the armed forces, like other professional services, are trained to carry out a job they hope they will never have to do. In their case, this means preparing to fight the enemies of their country. In addition, they give aid to the civilian community in times of crisis such as disasters and accidents, floods, air crashes and national strikes. In Northern Ireland where their task is to assist the police against terrorism and acts of violence they become targets for gunmen and rioters. They also help in hostage situations, shootings and in defusing bombs.

The most stressful situation for them is usually in time of war and when on duty in Northern Ireland. Terrorist activity also means that wherever they are stationed, whether in the United Kingdom or abroad, their wives and families, like those of the Royal Ulster Constabulary, are seen as 'legitimate targets'. Further stresses are caused by long periods of separation where it is not unusual for some to be away from their families more than nine months out of each year. They can move around frequently, especially in the army, disrupting their home lives and affecting schooling, friends, neighbours and work opportunities. When they are stationed abroad, wives have little or no access to their own families back home in times of need. They do have the support of Families' Officers, chaplains, doctors, Army Welfare Assistants, social workers and the regimental and unit family system, but the traumatic effects of all the pressures in the lives of service personnel, no matter how minor, spread out to affect wives and children.

Although many soldiers feel that when they are in Northern Ireland they are doing a useful job, they also face the fear of death or injury every day, separation from their families and sometimes extreme verbal and physical abuse and violence from the very people they are there to protect. They perform their duties in the belief that they are protecting society from the activities of terrorists and they approach their work with dedication and a strong element of good humour, even though they might recognize that this is a defence mechanism for coping with the feelings aroused in them.

The wars in the Falklands and Gulf resulted in a further area of stress in that many members of extended families suffered anxiety and looked for support and help because a son, daughter, brother, sister or other relative was serving there. In some cases, members of the armed services, and other organizations, have to face the death of a friend or colleague and this can result in a group as well as a personal loss. The death of someone in a unit can cause grief to many others, including those in the chain of command, and those in positions of authority may feel guilty and responsible. This can cause even stronger reactions of denial, for senior officers and senior ranks can react by believing that because they bear the responsibility they should remain strong for the sake of their men and not show any signs of weakness.

A young, but fairly senior officer who had commanded men in a war situation attended a church service where the chaplain spoke of the lack of responsibility and care in some of those in command in certain situations during the First World War. Whatever the point of the sermon, this officer, who could only just remember the Second World War as a boy, objected strongly to the criticism and took it personally. He said that some of his men had been killed and that it hadn't been his fault. He was in quite a state of agitation and he was having difficulty in coming to terms with the fact that when he had been in command some of his men had lost their lives. He was torn between what he saw as his responsibilities as a commander who should remain strong and unmoved, and his personal sense of grief, loss and possible failure.

Commanders in all organizations quite naturally can become very defensive about their responsibilities and decisions, especially when people are hurt or killed. The response can be to say that it wasn't their fault, that they were only doing their duty, and that someone had to make the decisions. This may cause strong reactions of denial of feelings with the result that they decide that they, or their men, do not need help. In some cases the response is to say that there have not been any reactions of stress or loss. If any reactions are admitted, then they must be from those who cannot cope and who should not be doing the job in the first place. This further strengthens the macho image, but can result in repressed emotions and more problems at a later stage.

The organization of the armed services provides an excellent basis on which to build a counselling and debriefing system, for extensive welfare support already exists. However, because of this system and the macho image that is common, it is easy to believe that Psychological Debriefing is not necessary. This image is very strong, not only at the bottom, but throughout the services, where it can produce the response that only 'wets and wimps' need help. Also, if the tendency is to believe that only those who have personality defects or are inadequate need help, there can be a strong feeling that any support should be provided through the psychiatric services and so a medical and psychiatric model is used. If people show signs of stress or trauma, they should be sent to see a doctor and a psychiatrist should be consulted. When an incident occurs, the system can mean that those in command look at the responses of the people involved and then decide who does and who does not need help. The danger in a hierarchical and disciplined organization can be that those in command feel responsible and therefore must make the decision, not only about who needs help, but also as to who should give it.

'Seven of my men were involved in a bombing where one of them was killed. The rest were all injured. Four seem to be coping well, but two are extremely upset and, of these, one is almost overcome with grief. Therefore, these two must see a psychiatrist, but the others are all right and just need to see a doctor.'

The problem with this, as has been said previously, is that it is not possible to make this kind of judgement. The copers might be the ones who are reacting strongly, whereas those who appear calm may not be able to keep their feelings locked inside for ever and at a later stage it may affect their work, health or families. It is much more effective to have Psychological Debriefing as standard operating procedure for everyone. None will be labelled as needing psychiatric care, for their responses will be seen as normal and they do not have the humiliation of having to ask for help. Should they need further help, they can seek assistance from a doctor, psychiatrist, community psychiatrist nurse or therapist.

The argument of this book is that the helping model should not be medical or psychiatric, but multidisciplinary and carried out by specially trained personnel. Each area, district or command could have a team of selected and trained debriefers, centrally supported and funded, who can be called upon whenever there is a critical incident. The armed services could do this easily with little cost and enormous benefit to the personnel concerned. Also, the public image of the services regarding support for those suffering from psychological and emotional problems, which has come under criticism, following the Falklands and Gulf Wars, would be enhanced and the response to combat, war and other traumatic incidents brought into line with that of many other Western armies.

Fortunately, there is a growing awareness in the armed forces of the reactions to traumatic situations and a great deal has been and is being done to help those who suffer from post trauma stress. Each of the services has a group of psychiatrists and clinical psychologists who specialize in traumatic stress and in helping those who suffer. Also, during and following the Gulf war a multidisciplinary team was created and trained to carry out Psychological Debriefing with those who had been held hostage and with the Graves' Registration Team. It is hoped that this debriefing will become standard procedure in the future, not just for those involved in war or Northern Ireland, but for any who suffer traumatic events.

The prison service

Prison officers live in a very special environment where men and women are forcibly separated from their families and the rest of society for long periods of time. The officers are also part of this system and usually work in an enclosed and disciplined community where there can be feelings of isolation, loneliness and threat. They move constantly between this environment and their own homes and, like the other services, can feel that they live in two separate worlds – the world of work where there is sometimes threat and violence and the world of their homes with their families where there should be freedom and normal family life.

They also are trained, but live under stress. It might be in relatively minor cases of frustration and anger or in the stresses of a full-scale riot like that at Strangeways in Manchester. This riot was partly the result of the conditions in the prison, such as overcrowding and the humiliations of 'slopping out', seen by prisoners as dehumanizing. There were also members of staff who believed this. Prison officers may have to live in a world where they are not happy about the conditions, but they have to make the best of it and carry out their duties efficiently and effectively.

The riots at Strangeways showed that in some cases there was an extremely strong sense of identification on the part of the staff, not just with their colleagues and the prisoners, but with the prison itself. Strangeways represented their whole lives and livelihood and they had dedicated themselves to their work to the extent that the riots and subsequent destruction of part of the prison buildings meant a deep personal loss for them. It was as though part of themselves had been ripped out or, like the prison, torn down. Trust and co-operation had been built up and then broken. In some members of staff, this caused strong reactions typical of post-trauma stress and there have been recent reports in the press of officers who were there suffering emotional, health and marriage problems.

Prison officers are trained to deal with riots, but they also have to cope with a fairly high level of stress in other areas of their work. They can face intimidation and threat, not always offered in an overt way, and anxieties about their own and the prisoners' living and working conditions. There can also be stress because of the difference between their work and home environments. Sometimes they have to cope with suicide or murder or violence between inmates and they may have problems in accepting and looking after certain types of prisoners. When they do face traumatic incidents they will need support and help during and following the event. This can be provided through their own chaplaincy and welfare services, but also through Psychological Debriefing.

The media

Newspaper and television reporters also face stress in their work, for wherever the above services are to be found, there are members of the press, looking for news and stories. Obviously, this news or story involves pain and loss for other human beings. Media people are also human beings, and the incidents they deal with can cause trauma and stress for them. Photographers and reporters in situations of war, disasters, accidents, deaths, murders, droughts, famine, floods, tornadoes, robberies, acts of terrorism and other sensational and dramatic events must be affected in some way, no matter how immune they might think they have become. Like others, they can retreat behind the screen of professionalism and of getting the job done, but there is no doubt that some reporters are deeply influenced by their experiences. We only have to think of some who went to Ethiopia and Africa and returned so deeply affected by what they saw that they were instrumental in raising money for famine relief. Some who took part in the Falklands and Gulf Wars have also said that their lives will never be the same again.

Sometimes there is criticism of the involvement of media photographers and reporters during and after traumatic incidents and it has even been alleged that some have dressed as clergy or doctors in order to gain access to victims and information. It may be that the stresses of their work sometimes push them to do things they wouldn't normally do. Such allegations may or may not be true, but it needs to be asked whether or not the involvement of the media is helpful or harmful to victims, survivors and rescue workers.

Obviously, there can be occasions where onlookers, by-standers, and other would-be helpers may prevent rescuers from doing their work. Similarly, the activities of photographers and reporters can sometimes be intrusive and disruptive. However, survivors and relatives can be helped by the knowledge that others are interested in and care about their problems and troubles, especially when the story, with photographs, reaches the daily or local papers, the radio or the television news. Publicity can also result in very positive responses from governments and organizations when injustices have been done, and many have been helped because a newspaper has taken up their case and cause. It can be that after an accident or disaster, or an event such as a murder, suicide or death, the press can help survivors and relatives to receive compensation or the satisfaction of knowing that something might be, or is being, done.

The problem can be that survivors of accidents and disasters, and parents and relatives, are often in a very delicate and fragile state because they are suffering from shock and symptoms of hysteria or numbness. Their reactions and feelings can be dulled so that they agree to be interviewed or give information shortly after the event, or they may actively seek and demand attention and publicity, all of which they might regret later. Occasionally, their response will be of extreme anger at what they see as an intrusion into their personal and private grief and suffering.

A sensitive press can help sufferers to know that others care, but a sensationalist press can do much damage and cause a deepening of the trauma for survivors and their families through their intrusion and sometimes aggressive behaviour in the pursuit of newsworthy items.

In the field of post-trauma stress, the press, radio and television have been instrumental in raising public interest and concern, especially after the Falklands and Gulf Wars and because of the plight of the hostages in the Middle East. Much publicity was given to the return of the hostages and of their need for help, understanding and debriefing. This has caused an interest in all of the public sectors and services and the realization that people can and do suffer from post-trauma stress and need help.

A major step in my life was a programme on the television some years ago made by Esther Rantzen about the effects of stillbirths on mothers and fathers. Many similar programmes on subjects such as bereavement and loss, child abuse and rape and the effects of accidents and disasters on ordinary human beings, have changed the attitudes of people at all levels. The media therefore have a great responsibility not only to bring news to the public mind and eye, but also because what they do and produce can influence the attitudes and opinions of everyone.

These are only a few of the organizations and services whose members face stress and trauma in their work. Much could be said about lifeboat personnel, air-sea and mountain rescue teams, coal-miners, oil-rig workers, merchant seamen, doctors and nurses, clergy and those who work for Relate, Victim Support, Cruse, the Samaritans, the Red Cross and St John's Ambulance, social workers, teachers, counsellors and many others whose work sometimes means encountering tragedy and loss. They can be exposed to the same stresses and traumas as those in the services mentioned above and have the same or similar reactions both from themselves and from their superiors. All need to be aware of the affects of critical and traumatic incidents on themselves and on others and of methods of coping.

Husbands, wives and partners

When we ask 'Who is involved?', it needs to be kept clearly in mind that we must include spouses and partners. It is easy to forget this and think only of the immediate victims and rescuers. Many of these have wives, husbands or partners and will return to them once the incident is over. Those who are not married or who do not have partners still have families, friends and colleagues. Some of the cases mentioned in this book show clearly that partners and children of victims and helpers are involved and influenced by the trauma.

Louise was sitting watching the television late one evening when the news suddenly reported live from the scene of a terrorist incident. To her horror, she saw her husband being carried on a stretcher to an ambulance. The immediate effect on her was one of shock and disbelief.

She went through the procedure of being officially informed that he had been injured and that one of his colleagues had been killed. She then had to visit him in hospital and go through the long and slow process of recovery once he returned home to convalesce. He had to cope with the trauma of the incident and the injuries he suffered, plus the death of his friend. He also felt guilty about having survived when his friend had been killed and the fact that he was now out of work and an invalid at home. His wife had to try to come to terms with her own shock and depression and her feelings of anger and resentment. Both had to cope with their own feelings as well as those of their partner.

The victim or survivor and the rescuer and helper are at the centre of the incident, but they are surrounded by those nearest to them in their families. All will be influenced in some ways by the event.

Wives and families of helpers can believe that the husband or father should be able to cope because 'that's his job and he should be used to it'. Wives and husbands of victims and helpers can become bored, angry, annoyed, apathetic and irritated by the behaviour of their partner.

The effects on relationships have been listed earlier in chapter 4 and in Appendix C, but the following are of special note.

- An inability or unwillingness to discuss things resulting in blazing rows and arguments or a retreat into isolation.
- The relationship can become very uncertain because life seems unpredictable, like the partner.
- There can be constant anxiety and worry about money, security and the future.
- Either one or both can discover an increased or decreased desire for physical affection.
- Partners can blame themselves and believe that it is their fault, or they may blame the other person. This can cause guilt and shame and feelings of being useless, rejected and unable to help.
- The anger and frustration can build up and explode and be directed at the other person, at children or at someone or something else.
- Panic is not uncommon, especially when people feel so helpless, and there may even be bouts of excessive spending or meanness.
- Partners can change and develop a new self-image or seek a new way of life.

The problem is that like the reactions to grief and loss, traumatic responses can have both a negative and positive effect. Some will deepen their relationships and need for each other and draw nearer in their care and concern, while others will drift apart and search for more satisfying or less demanding relationships.

Children

How do children react to trauma in themselves and in response to trauma in other family members? Sometimes it is difficult or impossible for them to say how they feel so they find other ways of showing or expressing their feelings.

Play

Children seem to find it easier to act out their feelings through what they do and in how they behave rather than in what they say. Some will become uncharacteristically aggressive in the way they play their normal games and in their relationships with their friends. In addition, they might even invent or find new games to play, especially games involving violence, such as playing soldiers or war games, being involved in an accident or taking on the role of someone in authority such as a policeman, soldier or doctor.

One little boy, four years of age, who had been involved in a hostage situation where his father was still being held, was playing with Lego pieces and he had a little Lego figure of a man with a large number of small white blocks attached to his head. When he was asked what had happened, he said that it was a man who had been hurt and that the blocks were bandages on his head.

He was too small to explain his fears, so probably acted them out in this way.

Other children can retreat into their own world, becoming quiet and uncommunicative, lose their appetite, play on their own or in their own rooms and shun contact with friends. They might also be aggressive with parents or destroy toys or other play things and be demanding and disruptive.

Another way of expressing how they feel can be through drawings or paintings.

A little girl whose father was away in the Gulf War, had drawn her own picture of 'daddy as a soldier' and she put this picture on her bed-side table in front of his photograph. She told her mother that the picture would only be taken away 'when daddy comes home'.

She was acting out her anxiety and worry in this small, but dramatic way. Others will draw or paint violent situations such as accidents or people fighting, or produce paintings with themes suggesting anxiety and worry or anger and sadness. Some psychologists specialize in art therapy with children who have been involved in trauma or who are suffering because of another member of their family.

Expressing feelings

These can be shown through play, drawings and unusual behaviour, but, as well as worry and anxiety, children can blame themselves. This can happen after accidents and disasters, but also because of other changes in life such as a divorce or separation or the death of a sibling, friend or other family member. Children can project problems between their parents outside onto others, or direct them internally through a process called introjection where they may blame themselves and believe that it is their fault. This can result in withdrawal or anger and in the need to be punished by being naughty or disruptive in the home or school.

Anxiety can be shown through an extra sensitivity to criticism from parents, friends or teachers. It is helpful for parents to know that this behaviour is not abnormal, but is a reaction to inner turmoil. Children may need more hugs and cuddles than normal. They need reassurance that they are still loved, and still loveable. Some will accept this love and caring, but others might reject physical contact or comfort and this can be very difficult for parents to cope with or accept.

Children might also complain of minor illnesses such as tummy-aches, headaches and feeling tired, or an inability to relax or sleep, or not want to go out or go to school. Even older children might return to an old teddy bear or toy from the past or to some pattern of previous childhood behaviour such as thumb sucking, clinging to a parent, crying or, in some cases, wetting the bed. They may also have bad dreams or nightmares. Teachers have reported children behaving in unusual ways when they have been involved in incidents or when a parent has been in an accident or disaster or, if a serviceman, away in a war or in Northern Ireland. It can also happen to children of others under stress from their work such as policemen, fire and rescue personnel, ambulance staff, prison officers and members of the helping professions and organizations. Any changes in behaviour can be significant, but should not always be seen as abnormal. They are responses to stress.

These and other reactions can be found not only in children involved in accidents, or disasters, or divorce or when a family member is suffering or has died, but also when some major change is about to or has taken place. These include losing a pet or friend, moving home or school or going into or coming out of hospital. It is a fairly common misconception that children do not suffer grief or loss, but they are as much at risk as anyone else, except that they might not be able to say or express how they feel.

Those involved closely with children as parents, family members or teachers will need to be more sensitive to their needs and reactions and, if possible, provide reassurance, security, comfort and understanding.

The problem with helpers

Helpers have two main problems, first they must do something and second, if they can't do anything they can feel a sense of failure.

Those who are not trained in counselling can especially feel that they have to be seen to be doing something, and if they can't they may feel redundant and useless. This can also be a problem for those who are, or believe that they are, in positions of authority and leadership. They may feel that they should have the answers or solutions to problems because of who and what they are and also because others expect this from them. Clergy and doctors particularly spring to mind.

Traditionally, clergy and doctors have been looked up to by others as people who have access to special authority and to solutions, whether from God or from some fount of all healing and knowledge. It can be difficult for them, and others in similar positions, to face situations where they feel, or are, helpless. There is nothing they can do except to stand back and wait, or to pray, and even this can eventually be thought of as a pointless and futile exercise – because it isn't seen to be *doing* something.

One method of coping, typical of stress reactions, is through denial. Professionals can easily retreat behind their roles and erect barriers which keep people and their problems at a distance. The clergy can hide behind a clerical collar and retreat into ritual and ceremony and the authority of their office. Doctors can use their professional status, the white coat and stethoscope, the hospital organization or the receptionists as a shield.

When talking about counselling and debriefing, a priest said:

> I don't need any of this counselling or debriefing nonsense. Whenever I come across any pastoral situation where there is a problem, be it a death, marital or personal problem, I take with me two thousand years of Christian spirituality.

Another responded by saying:

> I don't use any of this counselling or debriefing. My job is to preach the gospel wherever I am. That's what I do.

Both responses avoid the issue and threat of real involvement and helping by retreating behind the barriers of the Church, the priesthood and the gospel.

In the stage play *Whose life is it anyway?*, the doctor, chaplain and hospital social worker all come in for criticism because they treat the patient, Ken, an artist, who is paralysed from the neck down, as an object and not as a human being. They all hide behind their professional cloaks. The doctor believes that he can make decisions for him and force him to have injections; the chaplain tells him that he should be grateful that he's a cripple because others will feel good when they help him; and when he becomes angry and abusive, the female social worker talks about the decoration of the room. They all avoid the reality of the situation and of being involved.

When they are involved following accidents and disasters or bereavement, loss or any traumatic events, both clergy and doctors need to remind themselves that they also are human beings. They can help best, not by retreating into their own perceived professionalism, but by:

- being there and showing that they care;
- using their own professional skills and knowledge;
- understanding how trauma and loss affect individuals, families and themselves;
- developing the skills of listening and responding to those in need;

- being aware of the method of helping through psychological debriefing;
- knowing that if they have the time and the skills, clergy and doctors can either carry out the debriefing sessions themselves, or refer people to others who can.

I would return to the incident mentioned earlier in the book of the young man in hospital following a car accident in which his best friend was killed. He was told by the doctor and chaplain in the hospital that it hadn't been his fault and therefore he must not blame himself. He should put it behind him and get on with his life without any feelings of guilt, shame or anger. Had they been able to use, or find someone who could use, the skills of Psychological Debriefing they would have been more helpful and the young man would almost certainly not have been suffering to the same extent weeks later.

After accidents, disasters and other traumatic incidents, survivors, and in some cases their families with them, should be debriefed, either in hospital, at home or elsewhere and this should be part of the standard procedure and response.

How do rescuers and helpers cope?

Rescuers and helpers of all kinds have strategies for coping with the experience of being involved in traumatic incidents. These strategies are largely defensive and enable them to carry out their work effectively and, where possible, save lives. This must be their first task. However, they are not always aware of these strategies, but there is information and research which shows how some helpers have coped at the time of the incident and later. Although the paper discussed here concerns working with traumatized children, it should be of interest to all who help in other incidents, and the strategies used are similar.

Following a bus crash in Norway in August 1988, in which twelve children and three adults were killed, Atle Dyregrov and J. T. Mitchell produced a report entitled, *Work with Traumatized Children – Psychological Effects and Strategies for Coping.* The reactions are typical of carers and rescuers in other situations although the point is made very strongly that dealing with dead or traumatized children is especially stressful.

Seeing the bodies of dead children leads to significant emotional distress even in the most experienced helpers. But even in more routine work in hospitals, dealing with traumatized children intensifies stress in the worker.

A questionnaire was sent to all who worked at the site of the accident asking them about their responses and how they coped. It also asked for information about their role at the time, their previous experiences of accidents, if any, and their reactions during the first few weeks following the incident. This report is significant and important for those who work in situations of trauma and stress and can throw some light and understanding on personal and group methods of coping.

Coping strategies

- *Being active*   94 per cent believed that by doing something and keeping themselves busy they were able to curtail their feelings and prevent them from thinking about what they were doing. It was significant, but logical, that during rest periods or when they were trying to relax, this strategy didn't work because thoughts and feelings began to come to the surface.
- *Mutual support*   90 per cent mentioned the importance of the support they received from their friends and others at the site. This was particularly through close physical contact. Touching each other and talking were important for them and raised their morale.
- *Suppressing emotions*   76 per cent said that they were able to make conscious efforts to suppress their emotions and shut out their feelings.
- *Unreality*   68 per cent reported that the shock was experienced in very strong feelings of unreality. Most were unaware at the time that this enabled them to cope. If it was unreal, then they could carry on. One person said that he felt 'like an actor in a movie'.
- *Avoidance*   68 per cent said that they purposely avoided thinking about what they were doing and emotionally detached themselves from what they saw. Some even thought of the children as dolls in a training session.
- *Preparation*   63 per cent tried to prepare themselves for the event once they had been told they were to help, but some imagined that they would be dealing largely with old people.

The fact that they might have to deal with children was not in their minds and came as a shock. However, they did feel that mental preparation had helped them to cope.

- *Knowing what to do* 48 per cent said that their training helped them to cope because they felt competent and capable and knew what to do. This reassured them and raised their morale.
- *Regulating exposure* 38 per cent coped by limiting the amount of time they spent being actively involved. Some did not seek information, but preferred to remain in ignorance. What they did not know could not harm them. Some focused on one specific task at a time and avoided what was going on around them. Some also thought of something else, such as the garden at home.
- *Having a purpose* 24 per cent said that they thought that if they didn't do the work, then someone else, perhaps less skilled, would have to do it. This justified their involvement. There was also a sense of purpose and the knowledge that they were doing it to help the children.
- *Humour* 16 per cent said that they had used humour in order to cope and this is a much lower percentage than in other events.

These strategies are normal reactions, and they suggest that helpers and rescuers do have or develop internal methods for coping, some of them conscious and others unconscious. Training, preparation, acquired skills and previous experience are very important, plus a sense of solidarity, closeness with other helpers and mutual support. These mean that uniformed organizations with their own special training and the knowledge that they belong to an efficient and competent group are likely to cope better than those without any of these qualities. Everyone involved in critical incidents, including those responsible for training and support, should be aware of these strategies and strengths so that they can build on and develop them and be better able to cope under the traumas and stresses of their work.

Common reactions amongst helpers
Dyregrov and Mitchell report that although there were some reactions at the time, most helpers said that their main reactions only developed once they had left the site.

- *Helplessness*   67 per cent said that they felt almost completely helpless. This was difficult because their expectation as rescuers and helpers was that they should and would be in control. Working with children reminded them very starkly that they could do little or nothing to change what had happened. They felt that they should have been able to do more.
- *Fear and anxiety*   75 per cent of those who had children of their own or children they loved, felt especially vulnerable. They were frightened that the same thing might happen to their loved ones and they tended to become anxious and over-protective of their own children. In the Psychological De-briefing which followed the event, some said that they had to keep looking into their children's rooms to make sure that they were all right. There were also instances of this worry causing sleep disturbances.
- *Sense of unfairness and injustice*   The deaths of children are seen as 'a direct insult to a helper's assumptions of an orderly and just world. Since children are unable to protect themselves, their suffering is seen as unjust and unfair.' We expect our children to bury us, and not the other way around. A paper in 1988 by McCammon and others ('Emergency Workers' Cognitive Appraisal and Coping with Traumatic Events', *Journal of Trauma and Stress*, 1, 1988) shows that an important coping strategy amongst rescue workers and helpers is the search for meaning. Because the death of a child is out of sequence in life's expectations, it is difficult for it to make any sense.
- *Rage and anger*   Helpers and rescuers can direct anger and rage at those who seem to be responsible for the accident. Exposure to traumatized children can have other effects on helpers and carers who may become 'more critical, intolerant and less trustful of others' (Dyregrov and Mitchell). The ordinary problems of life can seem trivial and cause irritation, and the anger might be directed at families. This is rather similar to the response mentioned in an earlier chapter where a man was involved in a riot and his wife asked him if he wanted fish fingers and chips or beef burgers and chips. His response was one of anger for the question seemed irrelevant and trivial when compared with the trauma of his experiences.
- *Sorrow and grief*   Some helpers may become immune to the deaths of adults, but this is not true of those involved with

children where there can be responses of extreme sorrow akin to that of a personal bereavement. Crying was common and some said that when they went home and saw their own children, they immediately burst into tears. It is also significant that helpers will more readily accept crying and distress as a reaction to working with traumatized and dead children than with adults.

- *Intrusive images* When helpers, carers and rescuers are asked what incidents they remember from their experiences, they usually talk about having been involved with children. From this report it is evident that images and pictures were impressed on their minds. 'We carried two dead children in our ambulance. From one of the stretchers a leg with a yellow sock was visible. Now I see yellow socks everywhere.'
- *Self-reproach, shame and guilt* Many asked questions about how they performed their duties. Had they done enough and could they have done more or done it in a different and more effective way?

Positive results

More than 33 per cent said that as a result of the accident, their sense of value had increased and that life had become more precious to them. One year after the event, almost 45 per cent said that their lives had changed in meaning and they had come to appreciate their loved ones more, especially their children. They also said that they had been surprised at the strengths they had found in themselves and in others. Other reports produced after disasters and accidents produce similar findings (see Raphael et al, 1980).

Dyregrov and Mitchell say that helpers and carers are 'compassionate, dedicated and committed. They also have a great desire to be helpful to others.' These qualities mean that they have to help and therefore use conscious and unconscious strategies for coping. The main method of coping in an accident or disaster is to use 'emotional distancing' and when this does not work, for example in extremely distressing cases, it leads to the breakdown of natural defences. Coming across a dead child can cause these defences to collapse.

Also, carers and helpers tend to identify with victims, and especially with children. Instead of saying, 'It could have been me', they say, 'It could have been my child'.

It has already been said in an earlier chapter that childhood events can influence present responses, and some helpers when working with children unconsciously remember their own childhood separation anxieties and fears. The problem can be that helpers may see themselves more as substitute parents rather than rescuers or carers and this can have deeper emotional consequences.

The conclusion by Dyregrov and Mitchell is that rescuers, helpers and carers perform effectively, 'As long as they continue to be active, have concrete tasks to perform and are able to keep the emotional ramifications of the event at a distance.' This strategy of 'distancing' enables them to cope during the incident, but does not prevent reactions at a later time.

The use of humour

The paper also discusses the use of humour by helpers and the conclusion is that when dead or traumatized children are involved, humour is seldom used as a defence.

After the Piper Alpha disaster in the North Sea, Alexander and Wells (1990) found that 98 per cent of police officers working in the mortuary used humour as a defence in order to cope. In another paper, Hetherington and Guppy (1990) found that 93 per cent of police traffic officers also used humour as a coping mechanism.

This was not true in the Norwegian bus accident, because it involved children and also because onlookers and survivors were present. However, humour is a normal and helpful way of coping because it can 'reduce tension, keep emotional distance and build group cohesion and morale when performing arduous tasks' (Dyregrov and Mitchell). This seems to be a common method except in situations where children are involved. In the Norwegian accident, only 2 per cent said that they used it 'very much', 16 per cent said that humour was used in moderation, 24 per cent that it was used 'somewhat' and 60 per cent 'not at all'. When children are present in accidents or disasters, defences and reactions are stronger than usual, but the use of humour as a coping strategy is greatly reduced.

Dyregrov and Mitchell also say that talking about experiences and feelings with colleagues after the event was particularly helpful.

Clinical experience gained from providing follow-up debriefings for disaster workers in this and other accident and disaster situations highlights the need for confronting the event following the disaster work. While distancing is most helpful at the scene, the reverse seems to be most helpful afterwards. By actively confronting one's impressions and reactions through meetings and conversations with colleagues and others, the helper is able to manage the after effects of trauma work in the best possible manner. (Dyregrov and Mitchell)

This 'best possible manner' is through Psychological, or Critical Incident, Debriefing, which provides a structured method of talking through the experiences and feelings of those involved.

This debriefing should not be done on the day of the event or immediately the work is over.

During these times, many helpers still function in the emotionally distanced mode ... they need to change from reacting with their brain to reacting with both brain and heart. (Dyregrov and Mitchell)

This method of helping people to cope applies equally to survivors and, in some cases, will help families and others involved.

Therefore, the people involved in a traumatic incident can be someone falling off a horse, a person whose marriage has just broken down and their partner and children, a soldier returning from duty in Northern Ireland, a policeman who finds a mangled body in an accident, a fireman who rescues someone from a burning house, a counsellor with a client who was involved in a bombing, the friend and family of a young man who has committed suicide, or the victims and helpers in a major disaster. It can include all these people and those who come into contact with them, families and friends, neighbours and colleagues. Any or all of these are potential victims and may experience some of the symptoms of post trauma stress. They will need support, counselling, and debriefing.

Further reading

D. A. Alexander and A. Wells, 'Post Traumatic Stress Reactions among Police Officers after the Piper Alpha Disaster', un-published paper for the Second European Conference on Traumatic Stress, The Netherlands, 1990

Brian Clarke, *Whose Life is it Anyway?* (Amber Lane Press 1978)

A. Dyregrov and J. T. Mitchell, 'Work with Traumatized Children: Psychological Effects and Coping Strategies', in *Journal of Traumatic Stress* vol. 5 (1992)

A. Hetherington and A. Guppy, 'Post Traumatic Stress in British Police', unpublished paper for the Second European Conference on Traumatic Stress, The Netherlands, 1990

S. McCammon et al, 'Emergency Workers' Cognitive Appraisal and Coping with Traumatic Events', in *Journal of Traumatic Stress* vol. 1 (1988)

B. Raphael et al, 'Disaster – the Helper's Perspective', in *Medical Journal of Australia* 2 (1980)

8
Psychological Debriefing

After a situation which causes trauma and stress, a number of people will be involved, from a child falling off her bicycle and running to her mother, to large groups of people after a major disaster. This can include the victims and survivors, police, fire and rescue, ambulance services, doctors and hospital staff, witnesses and bystanders, voluntary helpers, counsellors, clergy, social workers, various community support services, British Red Cross and St John's Ambulance personnel, psychiatrists, psychologists and many others in an ever widening circle. At a later stage help and assistance might be given by Relate, the Samaritans, Cruse, the Compassionate Friends, Victim Support, the Citizens' Advice Bureau, and other organizations. In a minor incident only a few of these might be involved.

Jane crashed her car into a tree, but was not injured. She was interviewed by the Police and advised to consult a doctor, but apart from two pedestrians who stopped to see if they could help she did not speak to anyone else at the time. When she went home, she was able to talk about this to her husband and friends and they were sympathetic and helpful. Within a short time Jane was back to normal and driving again. However, she did drive extra carefully for some time afterwards.

In a major disaster, such as those at Zeebrugge and Lockerbie, large numbers of people were involved including relatives and friends and the general public. I can remember clearly where I was and what I was doing when President Kennedy was assassinated in 1963 and I can also remember that on March 6th 1987 I was at a party with some Australians when we heard about the Zeebrugge disaster. Because of instant media coverage, especially television, people in their homes can be brought to the scene of a disaster almost immediately. We have seen on television vivid and disturbing pictures of the incident when two soldiers were taken in Northern Ireland by a crowd and shot dead, the fire at Bradford, Hillsborough, the explosion at Flixborough near Hull in 1974, the earthquake in Mexico City in 1985, the fire at King's

Cross in 1987, and many others in this country and abroad. The pathetic sight of survivors and the devastation, destruction and carnage caused to people and places, a child's toy, a handbag or an article of clothing, or the bodies of victims, can bring strong emotional reactions from those who have no direct involvement other than watching a television screen in the comfort of their own homes. Any major incident can have effects which are like the ripples on a pond when a stone is thrown into the water. They spread out in a widening circle of influence, affecting all they touch, until the energy is gradually dispersed.

Methods of helping

There are a number of ways in which people can be helped to cope with traumatic events.

Self-help and awareness

There is self-help for victims, rescuers, helpers and others through knowledge, preparation and training.

Rescuers and helpers need to be trained, to cope not only with the incident, but also with their own and others' reactions at the time and later. Victims, survivors and their relatives can be helped by already knowing about post-traumatic stress reactions and by being aware that such responses are normal. General education on grief, loss, stress and trauma for everyone, including school children, is essential and can be done through the media, school, and training in the work-place. The methods discussed in chapter 6 of coping with trauma and loss, which are similar to those used in grief and loss reactions, will also be helpful for all.

Defusing

This is the procedure during the incident where there is mutual support and caring, and an opportunity after the event to gather informally to talk through what has happened.

Psychological or Critical Incident Debriefing

This is the main subject of this chapter and can be used with individuals, couples, families or groups. It is a process which should take place not less than 24 hours after the incident. The ideal time for a Debriefing is about 48 hours following the incident although it can be carried out much later than this, even after a number of weeks.

Post-Traumatic Stress Disorder

There are methods used particularly with those who are suffering from Post-Traumatic Stress Disorder and these are discussed at length in chapter 6 of *Coping with Catastrophe* by Hodgkinson and Stewart. They include:

- *Behavioural treatments* such as desensitization and exposure to the fear, flooding techniques and training in methods of relaxation.
- *Cognitive therapy* where the aim is to correct unreasonable, distorted and unhelpful beliefs.
- *Psychotherapy* which attempts to deal with the anxiety caused, the defence mechanisms generated and the feelings which are buried and hidden away.
- *Group therapy* which sometimes includes residential care and treatment.
- *Medication* which should normally be used in conjunction with the other methods mentioned above, and has been especially successful when combined with psychotherapy.

Initial problems

For those not suffering from Post-Traumatic Stress Disorder, where psychiatric or psychological help may be necessary, the most positive help lies in encouraging them to talk about their experiences and feelings to a good listener or counsellor and to have support and understanding from families, friends and colleagues at work.

However, there is a more structured method of assisting which is called Psychological Debriefing or Critical Incident Stress Debriefing. These raise a number of problems, not least in the implications of the titles.

Denial

One of the natural reactions to loss and stress already discussed is that many will deny that they, or others, have any problems. Therefore words like 'psychological' and 'stress' suggest the need for treatment and can strengthen the denial.

'I don't need help. I'm very well thank you.'
'My people are professionals. They are well trained and don't suffer from stress.'

Those involved in a traumatic incident and those responsible for them can use the defence of denial and say that they are coping and do not need help. It should be stressed that many will cope through their own inner resources and with the help and support of their families and friends, but it needs to be acknowledged that the effects might continue for some time and be buried deep inside.

The title

The words 'psychological' and 'stress' have various stigmas attached to them, even for those who would not deny that there is such a thing as stress or trauma. Also, to some people, 'psychological' suggests madness, nervous breakdown, being crazy, mental illness, instability, going out of your mind, insanity, weakness or character deficiency.

'I don't want anything to do with head-shrinkers. There's nothing wrong with me. I certainly wouldn't want that on my records.'
'I never suffer from stress. I can cope very well thank you.'
'I don't want to be labelled a head-case and I don't want to see any shrink or do-good counsellor.'

Following a hostage situation a number of people were offered debriefing, but it was described by the authorities as counselling and, understandably, the response of many was to say very firmly, 'No thank you, I don't want to be counselled. I don't need treatment.'

The word 'debriefing' is also a problem for some. In the armed services and other uniformed organizations it usually means a meeting, following an incident or exercise, concerned with either giving or obtaining information, or sharing ideas, experiences and opinions. There is not usually any reference to feelings or emotions. An interview carried out by the police after an accident or other traumatic event with a survivor or victim is largely concerned with finding out what has happened and what they can recall or remember. The problem can be that if someone is traumatized, it can either be difficult for them to remember, or the story just pours out like a flood. It might be very difficult to avoid the feelings. Often if you ask someone what they thought, they tell you what they felt; that's entirely different because they immediately switch into their emotions. In most cases the police are very aware of this, although it can be very difficult for the interviewer to remain detached enough to obtain the information without being overcome by the emotional content.

The suggestion is also made that the word 'counselling' should be used – Critical Incident Counselling – but counselling and psychological debriefing are not the same. Counselling is sometimes a long-term process whereas psychological debriefing, based on the Dyregrov and Mitchell model, is meant to be a one-off event carried out in a highly structured and disciplined manner with the possibility of a follow-up at a later stage. This will be discussed later.

Because of the above problems, some believe that it is easier if the process is referred to as Critical Incident Debriefing, for this avoids using the words psychological and stress, but here we will use the term Psychological Debriefing.

The method and model

There are difficulties to be faced whichever method or model is used for helping those who are involved in traumatic incidents. Some will refuse to talk about their experiences and feelings and will keep them locked up inside while others will talk for hours. Psychological debriefing is usually done in a group setting where everyone is given an opportunity to speak, but a few will find this very threatening and will not wish to meet or talk with others. They will avoid even those who shared the experience of the disaster with them. Some of those who feel like this may eventually talk, but they feel safer if it is with someone who is neutral, not known to them, not involved and not someone from their own organization or unit. It has already been said that some who are suffering stress or trauma will probably not want any peer group or those in authority to know in case it affects their image and future. To have debriefing as the usual and normal procedure for everyone, can put some of these fears at rest.

The Dyregrov and Mitchell model and method of Psychological Debriefing can be adapted for use after any traumatic situation, from a relatively minor accident to a major disaster. However, it is not concerned with the scale of the incident, but how people have reacted and what it has done to them. The model can also be used with an individual, with couples or with a larger group.

Who suffers?

Again, this has been previously mentioned; it needs to be kept firmly in mind that most will cope by using some of the various defence mechanisms discussed in chapters 5 and 6, but that all will feel the effects in some way. The denial of this means that there will be the belief that only those who are seen to be suffering will need help.

Looking at people is no certain way of determining who is or who is not suffering. Physical injuries are usually visible or detectable, but psychological stress and trauma can be well hidden and buried away. Those who are shouting and screaming and crying and talking might be the ones who are coping because they are able to express their feelings and emotions and bring them out into the open. Someone who is quiet and calm may be suffering inner turmoil and confusion and be keeping a firm grip on reactions of shock and horror.

Psychological Debriefing, if it is accepted as normal procedure, can surmount these problems because it is something which is intended for everybody involved and not just for those who *appear* to be suffering. A debriefing group will usually consist of some who are coping well, others who are having difficulties and a few who might have long-term problems. The message which needs to be repeated continuously until it is understood and accepted is:

PSYCHOLOGICAL DEBRIEFING IS FOR EVERYONE

Organizations and institutions should include Psychological Debriefing as the normal procedure for all who share in the traumatic experience. In the case of an accident or disaster, the most obvious people at risk are the survivors and those working at the site of the incident. Therefore, debriefing should be for survivors, rescue workers and helpers first as a priority, but the list can be even wider and those on the periphery of the incident may also benefit from debriefing. At the very least, they should know of the possible effects of what has happened to their relatives or friends and how this can influence them also. There are others who will feel the effects in some way and they are even further out in the circle. Starting at the centre and moving gradually outwards, a comprehensive list would be:

- *Survivors*
- *Helpers* – police, fire and rescue, ambulance services, etc.
- *Bystanders and witnesses*
- *Carers* – doctors, nurses, clergy, etc.
- *Families and friends* – work colleagues and neighbours
- *Debriefers and other helpers* – trained debriefers, Relate counsellors, Samaritans, Cruse, Victim Support, social workers and those from other caring agencies.

All will need some help and support, if not debriefing.

Defusing

It is essential that helpers are trained and prepared, as far as is possible, for critical and traumatic incidents. Their sense of belonging to a professionally trained group will help them as will the support they receive from each other before, during and after the event. They will use their own particular defences for coping at the time, but will be helped if they can talk to those working with them. Also it helps if they can gather for routine meetings to talk through their experiences during the incident and once it is over. This process is called *defusing* and creates an opportunity not only for them to talk to each other, but also for them to think about discussing their emotional reactions. At this stage they do not normally need professional counselling and the defusing can be done informally by some member of the team, possibly one of the leaders. The services of organizations like The Salvation Army in providing cups of tea or coffee and a cake or sandwich during the incident also give an opportunity to talk and share experiences and are a valuable element in helping people to cope. Clergy and medical staff can also be present and, as well as giving medical help or spiritual comfort, they can be useful in giving verbal and physical support, understanding and encouragement.

Immediately after the incident, those involved are often not in a fit state to be able to deal with their experiences so there should be no attempts to criticize and no excessive use of humour or boisterous behaviour. The Psychological Debriefing should not be carried out immediately, for people will not be able to cope with it. Dyregrov and Mitchell have said that at this stage victims, rescuers and helpers are thinking with their heads rather than with their heads and hearts. Preferably, the debriefing should take place after about 48 hours. It can be done later than this, but not so late that the feelings and emotions have become internalized and mixed up with other things.

Psychological debriefing

Psychological Debriefing can be defined as:

A meeting with one or more persons, the purpose of which is to review the impressions and reactions that survivors, helpers and others experience during or after a traumatic incident such as an accident or disaster. (Dyregrov, 1989)

The aim is to give an opportunity for people to talk and share their experiences and feelings, to reduce any after effects and also to minimize the possible development of symptoms of Post-Traumatic Stress Disorder.

The model of debriefing suggested here is that produced by Dr Atle Dyregrov of the Senter for Krisepsykologi (The Centre for Crisis Psychology), Solheimsvik, Bergen, Norway, following other work by J. T. Mitchell. The value of this model lies in its flexibility, in that it can be adapted to suit many different situations from a relatively simple incident involving one or two people to a major disaster.

The important elements in debriefing are as follows.

It is for all

Debriefing should be seen as the *normal* response to all who have been involved in a traumatic incident – survivors, witnesses, helpers and carers and, sometimes, their families. It should be standard procedure and the armed services, police, fire and rescue and ambulance services in particular, should have debriefing written into their operating instructions and orders.

A number of hostages who returned from overseas said:

When we stepped off the plane we expected three things. First, a medical to see if we were physically fit. Second, a normal debriefing about our experiences. Third, we wanted to talk about what we have been through and how we feel. We had the first two, but not the third.

For example, after a road traffic accident, a debrief could be carried out with the police officers involved, the ambulance personnel, and perhaps other helpers. This would probably be difficult to do because it would necessitate crossing the boundaries of different organizations, but, at the least, each group could have their own system of using debriefers. After a bank robbery, all those working in the bank could meet together for a general debrief. In the case of the chaplains meeting for a debrief after a riot, all the clergy attended, even those who were not there at the time, for they all felt that they were involved because they belonged to the team and had been drawn in emotionally throughout the incident and following it.

The here and now
The main focus of the debrief is on present reactions and feelings. This will result in discussing and looking at the incident, how it happened, what people saw and experienced and how they feel about it now.

Mobilizing resources

The multidisciplinary approach The approach to debriefing should be multidisciplinary and not labelled as the domain of any particular specialists. Post-trauma stress is not exclusively a medical, psychological, spiritual or social condition, but can contain elements of them all. It is important not to medicalize, psychologize, spiritualize or socialize it, for people can then assume that they are ill and feel that they need specialist help from a doctor, psychiatrist, priest or social worker. It should be done by those who are trained, whatever their other professional orientations or skills.

One solution to the problem would be to have a nationally organized and multidisciplinary team of trained debriefers who could be called upon when needed. They could be drawn from many organizations and disciplines, selected and then trained in the debriefing model. Often there is resistance from those in authority who might see this procedure as threatening their leadership capabilities or discipline.

The benefits of debriefing It can be pointed out, especially to those in positions of responsibility or who hold the purse strings, that debriefing has certain specific benefits. It can:

- reduce any short or long-term distressing after effects, particularly the development of Post Traumatic Stress Disorder;
- reduce the incidence of sickness and absenteeism;
- reduce personal, marital and relationship problems;
- reduce problems at work;
- reduce anxieties about how people might cope and what help they will receive after an event;
- reduce anxieties for any who might feel threatened or embarrassed if they had to ask for help;
- reduce anxieties about stress and traumatic reactions being thought of as signs of weakness.

Perhaps as important as any of these is the knowledge that the organization does care and is using techniques which will help. The positive spin-off in terms of time and money can be enormous and any company or organization should see the benefits of this process, even if they are not entirely visible or concrete.

Education It is also important that educational programmes be used for all members of staff, at all levels, so that they are aware of the possible reactions to stress and trauma. Leaflets and booklets can also be made available. Banks and Building Societies do have training sessions which prepare staff for occasions such as robberies and hold-ups, but should also include information on how these incidents might affect them.

Trained debriefers An essential resource must be the availability of professionally trained personnel to carry out the debriefings. These can be people from inside the organization, selected and trained, provided they meet the following requirements. They should:

- be carefully selected and trained;
- belong to a support group;
- be working under supervision with a tutor-consultant;
- be trained counsellors;
- have a knowledge of group structures and dynamics and experience of working with groups as well as with individuals or couples;
- have knowledge of post-trauma stress and the possible effects on individuals, groups and families;

- be thoroughly conversant with the debriefing model and know how to adapt it to their situation.

There will be some counsellors who might feel that they do not need all this and that their skills and experience should be sufficient for them to cope. However, debriefing is not the same as counselling. Counselling techniques and methods are used, but have to be applied within the formalized structure of the debriefing model. Normally, counselling involves a series of sessions, usually for a limited amount of time such as an hour, which can take place over a number of weeks or months, or even longer periods. Psychological Debriefing involves one or more sessions set within a formal structure carried out, at the earliest, within two to three days of the incident taking place. It can last for a morning or afternoon, for a day or longer. The debriefing with a team of chaplains after the Strangeways riots, was spread over two days and carried out in the relaxed surroundings of an old country house. The debriefing of a family held hostage took three hours. Debriefers may be consultants working on a part-time basis, whose advice is sought and who are called in when needed.

The Psychological Debriefing model

- Debriefing can be carried out by one debriefer, but two debriefers can be used to greater advantage, possibly one male and one female.
- Because the session is open-ended and might carry on for some time it is a good idea to ensure that all have paid a visit to the lavatory beforehand.
- Tea- and coffee-making facilities should be available.
- A rule should be agreed and established about smoking.
- They should sit around a table, all in similar chairs, including the debriefer. Being around a table rather than in an open circle removes the possible impression that they are attending a therapy session. An open circle is also much more threatening.
- No observers, press or others should be included.
- Group members should be told that if they wish to leave at any time they are to do so quietly, but this should be discouraged. They should be told that it will be a long session lasting some hours and without a break.
- When the group is gathered together in a place which is

suitably relaxing, comfortable and private the leader takes charge.

Introduction

After a short self introduction the leader, and co-debriefer, if present, talk about personal experiences of debriefing. This helps to create confidence at the beginning of the session.

The rules

The following rules are made clear.

- *You do not have to say anything* other than what your role was at the time and why you were there.
- *Confidentiality is emphasized.* There should be no note-taking, unless by mutual agreement. If notes are taken, a record of the meeting can be sent to members of the group afterwards. Nobody outside will be contacted without the permission of those in the group. Those taking part must agree not to talk to anyone outside about what happens in the group.
- *The main focus is on reactions now.* It is stressed that although past experiences and feelings will probably emerge, the main emphasis is on impressions and thoughts as they are expressed and felt in the group.
- *Feeling worse.* Those taking part should also be warned that they might feel worse during and after the session, but that this is normal.
- *Complaints.* It should be explained that the group is not a forum for dealing with complaints and moans – of which there will probably be many.

Procedure

Those taking part are then asked:

- How did you learn about the event?
- If you are a helper, what were you doing when you heard about the incident and how did this affect you?
- How did you come to be there?
- What was your role?

A natural method of doing this is to go around the group and ask each person in turn – beginning with the debriefer.

Expectations and facts

Responses to the previous questions should lead on to talking about the facts of the situation as each one saw, or sees them. Thoughts and expectations should be expressed for this gives an idea of how prepared, or otherwise, people were for what happened.

- Did you expect deaths and injuries?
- Did you expect to see mutilated bodies?
- Did you expect to see children suffering or dead?
- What did you expect to happen?
- What did you think at the time?
- Did you expect violence?
- How were you treated by others while you were there?
- How prepared were you for what happened?
- What did you think was happening?

Thoughts and impressions

When people in the group are describing what they saw and now see as the facts of the situation it should lead to such questions as:

- What were your first thoughts on becoming involved?
- What did you decide to do next?
- Why did you decide to do this?

The sharing of impressions and facts can help the group members to have different perspectives on what happened and therefore see their own involvement in a different light. Some of their thoughts will be confirmed by others in the group, but they might find that their impressions, perceptions and reactions were based on incorrect information.

This helps them to:

- put their own reactions into perspective;
- have a cognitive grip on the situation;
- share and integrate their own experiences;
- clarify their own and others' roles.

Having a 'cognitive grip' means that those involved will try to make sense of their experiences, reactions and feelings so that they can come to terms with them. The purpose of this section is to bring out the thoughts that are in their minds.

Sensory impressions are also important. What did they see, touch, smell, taste, feel?

Expressing sensory experiences helps people to prevent or control memories which might be triggered by external stimulants at some time in the future. A picture, sound, smell or taste can cause flash-backs (or flash-forwards), and bring the events into the present again. Talking these through helps the participants to be prepared to face any future experiences.

Emotional reactions

This is usually the longest part of the debriefing. Questions about expectations and facts, thoughts and impressions and sensory experiences invariably lead to answers describing feelings. 'What did you *think* about. . . ?' often receives the response, 'I *felt* that . . .'.

People will probably speak about some or all of the following which are typical symptoms of post-trauma stress. Their presence does not mean that those who have experienced them are ill or that Post-Traumatic Stress Disorder will develop.

> Fear Helplessness Frustration Self-reproach Guilt Anger Depression Hopelessness Shame Isolation Anxiety Bitterness Regret Blame Sadness Failure
> 'We are pawns in a terrible, sick game.'
> Nightmares and dreams Intrusive thoughts Feelings of aggression Irritability Unreality Senselessness Futility Conflict

Sharing feelings is important and the leader acts as a catalyst in allowing the feelings to be expressed. Some will talk a great deal and others will remain silent or have little to say. The leader should use skills to encourage all to participate as fully as they are able and not allow a few to dominate the session. By moving around the table, this should encourage everyone to take part.

Questions should be:

- What did you feel in the beginning?
- What did you feel later?
- How did your colleagues at work treat you and what did they say?

- What about others who were with you?
- How did it feel to be separated from your own family?
- What was the worst thing you experienced?
- Did you cry and when?
- Did you swear or become angry and when?
- What happened when you went home?
- How did your wife/partner/children/family/friends react?
- What did other people ask you about the incident, how did this make you feel and what did you say to them?

Some will react in ways which they can't explain, but find disturbing.

A man involved in a riot which lasted many days travelled home each night. One morning he woke up and thought that it was all a bad dream. He got into his car and drove down to where the incident was taking place and as he drew nearer he realized that it was true. He turned around in the car, went home and changed the sheets on his bed.

The reactions of other people can cause problems.

Ian, a soldier, returned from the Falklands War and found that his family had arranged a celebration party. He was hailed as a hero and some asked him how many 'Argies' he had killed. He became extremely angry and refused to attend the party. He said later that he saw this as an attempt to glorify war and he couldn't cope with it. Some of his friends had been killed and he had seen many Argentinian bodies. For Ian, there was no cause to celebrate. He spoke of the sheer horror and terror of the battlefield and contrasted this with the happy faces when he returned home. It made him physically sick.

In this section of the debrief there is often a very sharp contrast between the shattering experience of the event and the seemingly trivial questions and answers which are given in the group. Sometimes members of the group will recall previous experiences which they have found distressing. If some are distressed or cry during this stage, it is usual for others in the group to give support. A fairly strong feeling of sharing can develop so that when one is upset others will put their arms around them or offer verbal support. When someone is very upset, or cries, the debriefer can ask others in the group to support them. Final questions in this section can be?

• What do you feel as you sit here?
• What are you main worries and anxieties?

The leader should be aware of any who may need special help, but this should not be mentioned within the group. They can be approached privately afterwards or may ask for further help.

Normalization

Here the leader emphasizes that the reactions and feelings experienced are entirely normal. A brief explanation of post-trauma stress reactions should be given to reassure people that they are not stupid or going mad. The debriefer can also explain the effect this can have on their families. Dyregrov calls this stage 'anticipatory guidance'.

Future planning and coping

Here the possibility of needing help and support for themselves and their families is discussed.

• What help and support do you think you need now?
• What resources are available at work and at home for you, your family and colleagues?
• How will you deal with difficult people and situations?
• Do any of your family need to talk things through?
• What about any children at home or away at school who will have heard about the incident? What help can they be given?
• What have you learned from others in the group?

The leader can also outline sources of help and organizations they can call on for assistance. It should, again, be stressed that these are confidential. Some will feel very vulnerable at this stage and might resist any offers of help. They might see this as threatening them and their ability to survive.

Disengagement

This section gives an opportunity for any other questions to be raised. Further help should be offered on a confidential basis.

Members should also be asked to discuss whether or not they wish to meet again in the near future, and if so, when and with whom. Some will feel that they want to meet again, but others will not wish to do so – either because they are actually coping or because they are defending themselves by the use of denial.

Group members should be told that they might need help if:

- the symptoms do not begin to decrease after four to six weeks, or longer in a personal case of loss or bereavement;
- symptoms increase over time;
- there is a loss of function or ability at home, with the family or at work or elsewhere;
- marked personality changes occur.

They should know where to go for help and a list of confidential and other telephone numbers can be handed out, although some might not wish to take one.

Follow-up

There may or may not be a follow-up after the debriefing. Some debriefers would see this as a necessity whilst others would think that it should only be done when the nature and extent of the incident and the effect on those involved requires it. If it is a 'minor' incident, then a follow-up should not be necessary and the debriefing session should be sufficient.

Two things need to be kept in mind. First, those being debriefed must be reassured that their reactions are normal and nothing should be said or done which might suggest that they are ill, will get worse or need constant help and support. The debriefing session will help them to cope and reduce the possibility of deeper symptoms emerging. Second, a follow-up, if presented as the normal and usual procedure, can help to check-out reactions and confirm their progress. They will also know that there is support, should they need it.

The debriefer can then say that the normal procedure is that after about a month they will be contacted confidentially to confirm their progress. At this stage, some might say that they do not wish to be contacted. The debriefer should accept this as a normal reaction, for some people, to the debriefing.

Summary

The leader then gives a brief summary of what has happened in the session, and can make the offer of further help for any who might need it. The group can then disperse.

The provision of coffee or tea and sandwiches can provide an opportunity for less formal discussion although some might wish to leave immediately. Others will stay and talk.

The debriefer may leave at this stage and this can confirm the feeling that the debriefing has been carried out and that the session is now over. Some debriefers will wish to stay and talk, but they should not ask questions about or discuss the session unless they are asked.

Conclusion

What should be kept firmly in mind is that the process of Psychological Debriefing will help the recovery of people who have experienced abnormal events in their lives.

It is also important to realize that this kind of debriefing is not something carried out on a weekly or monthly basis. There might be a series of sessions on one day or over a few days, but they are intended as part of one continuous process. When the debriefing is over, the debriefer might not have any further contact with the members of the group. If they wish to form a support group and meet together, this is something they should organize themselves. What must be avoided is giving any impression that their reactions and present state are unusual or abnormal. If this happens, they might believe that they are ill, weak or inadequate. The debriefer should feel:

'My job is now over and I have done sufficient to help these people to cope with their feelings and emotions. They should now be able to face their families, friends and colleagues with a degree of confidence. If they have problems they know where they can find help. I have not made them feel that they are pathetic or weak.'

Debriefers will need to be debriefed themselves and talk it over with a colleague or supervisor. They will be left with much unpacked luggage which they have collected from the group and they will probably be concerned about how the group, or certain individuals in it, are coping.

The debriefers

Those who carry out Psychological Debriefing must be carefully selected and trained. If not, they could do immense harm. Debriefing must not be done by those who think that they can do it without any training or support.

Those selected as debriefers should become familiar with the model and method of debriefing and should practise it through role-play. They should attend a course which would consist of the following essential elements.

- Checking initial listening and counselling skills.
- Explaining post-traumatic stress reactions and effects on individuals, families and groups.
- Introducing group dynamics.
- Role-play, preferably with closed-circuit TV.
- Discussion of any problems or questions.
- Support for debriefers.

General comments

Psychological Debriefing is an essential part of the process in helping people to cope with the after effects of post-trauma stress and to prevent the development of Post-Traumatic Stress Disorder. It should include *all* those who have been involved including victims, survivors, carers and helpers.

The method and model evolved by Atle Dyregrov and J. T. Mitchell can successfully be adapted for use with people following:

accidents	robberies
disasters	divorce and separation
shootings	bombings
hostage situations	rape
war and combat	acts of violence.

It can also be used after particularly distressing events involving bereavement and loss such as suicides, murder and multiple deaths and also lengthy, unsuccessful rescue attempts.

Those in authority should ensure that it is not viewed as an optional extra, but is included as a normal part of the response to accidents and disaster. It should be standard operating procedure and written into the rules.

There should be a nationally organized and funded body to provide teams of debriefers who can be called upon when needed and who can give advice and help. This team should be multidisciplinary and the personnel selected and trained.

Following the hostage situation before the Gulf War, a team of debriefers was formed consisting of clergy, social workers, welfare assistants and hospital welfare personnel. All had considerable counselling experience. Some felt unable to use the Psychological Debriefing model and chose to act in a supporting role, either within the debriefing groups or outside with children and other family members. They were also able to help those who chose to leave the groups during the sessions. This team was supported and assisted by a leader, two psychiatrists and a clinical psychologist, all of whom were experienced in the process of Psychological Debriefing.

Such a group of debriefers could be organized and trained, either nationally or locally and be made available when there are traumatic incidents. Many organizations could have their own counsellors trained in Psychological Debriefing or should be able to call upon professional debriefers or consultants from outside.

There should also be a process of education for all carers and helpers and those in positions of leadership and authority. This could be done nationally with the help of government, local authorities (health, education and social service departments), the armed forces, the police, fire and rescue and other local and county services. Voluntary organizations should also be involved and included. All these organizations, especially those involved in counselling, can include awareness training on post-trauma stress reactions and some counsellors could be trained as debriefers.

Victims and helpers who suffer the effects of trauma, whatever the cause, will need to be supported as far as is possible, during and following the event. While the incident is taking place, this support is known as 'defusing', and consists of the usual and familiar responses. These will include:

- being aware of the coping mechanisms operating;
- giving verbal and physical support;
- allowing periods of rest;
- providing medical attention and counselling support.

Once the incident is over, the 'defusing' should continue. For helpers and carers this will normally consist of:

- a debriefing meeting with those in charge when immediate experiences and practical problems can be discussed;
- medical examinations if necessary;
- brief counselling support;
- a period of rest, and a return to work.

This 'defusing' will depend on the nature of the event and whether or not it is for a victim or helper.

Some members of staff in a bank were involved in an armed robbery. After the incident was over, they were sent for a medical check-up and given some time off work. The area manager called to see them and they received letters of support and bunches of flowers. Counselling was made available, but all declined the offer.

The victim of a traffic accident was taken to hospital where she was given excellent medical attention and lots of 'tender loving care' by the nursing staff. She was given reassurance by the nurses, doctors and the chaplain, and her family visited regularly, bringing the inevitable bunches of grapes and flowers. On leaving hospital a few days later, she was allowed a few days rest and then returned to work.

Such 'defusing' is excellent and necessary and is normal practice for most occasions, but is not sufficient. Psychological Debriefing, carried out by trained staff some two days or so after the event, and in some cases much later, will enable the victims or helpers to talk through the incident in an informal but structured way. It provides a forum for them to talk about their impressions, reactions and feelings and, through sharing with the group, helps them to make some kind of sense of what they have experienced. It will reduce tensions and feelings of abnormality and encourage them to mobilize and utilize their own resources and those of the group and organization to which they belong. It will also prepare them for any future reactions. Above all, it reassures them that they are normal people reacting in normal ways to an abnormal experience. Spouses or partners can also be included in the debriefings. If not, they should certainly be made aware of the nature of the incident and the possible effects upon them and the relationship. The effects on any children in the families also needs to be considered.

By having such help and support available through Psychological Debriefing, those who experience traumatic events can be helped to carry on more successfully with their lives. This is not an optional extra or luxury for a few. Neither is it only for those who appear to suffer or for those who request it. It is a necessary and essential element in any response to those who experience trauma of any kind. Without Psychological Debriefing, some will suffer unnecessarily and a few will experience long-term problems, even months or years later. The benefits for individuals, families, groups and society in general are inestimable. We should let Atle Dyregrov have the last word.

> By providing survivors, bereaved and helpers in disasters with rapid help, and by building on the internal strengths of the affected groups, we may prevent much of the unnecessary pain and agony experienced by these groups.

> I certainly hope that we can prevent post-traumatic stress reactions in the future, not only by psychological debriefings, but by a better system for intervening in crisis situations. Hopefully debriefings in addition to other measures can accelerate normal recovery and prevent post traumatic stress disorder. (Dyregrov 1989)

Further reading

Bruno Bettelheim, *The Informed Heart* (Pelican 1988)
A. Dyregrov, 'Caring for Helpers in Disaster Situations: Psychological Debriefing', in *Disaster Management* 2 (1989)
A. Dyregrov, *Critical Incident Stress Debriefing* (University of Bergen, Norway)
P. E. Hodgkinson and M. Stewart, *Coping with Catastrophe* (Routledge 1991)
J. T. Mitchell, 'When Disaster Strikes', in *Journal of Emergency Medical Services* (1983)
Psychological Aspects of Disaster (British Psychological Society 1990)
B. Raphael, *When Disaster Strikes* (Hutchinson 1986)

Address
Dr A. Dyregrov
Senter for Krisepsykologi (Centre for Crisis Psychology)
Fabrikkgaten 5
5037 Solheimsvik
Bergen
Norway

Appendix A
THE PSYCHOLOGICAL
DEBRIEFING PROCESS

Introduction
Introduce self and explain the rules.
    You don't need to speak.
    Confidentiality inside and outside the group.
    Emphasis is on the here and now.
    Explain that they might feel worse to begin with but that this is normal.
    The debrief is not a forum for complaints.
Expectations and facts
    What did you expect would happen?
    What did happen?
    What did you see and experience?
    What were your thoughts at the time?
    Did you expect violence, dead bodies & carnage?
    How were you treated by others?
Thoughts and impressions
    What were your first thoughts?
    What did you decide to do and why?
    What were your impressions then and now?
    What did you see, hear, smell, touch, taste?
Emotional reactions
    Thoughts lead to feelings.
    What was the worst about what happened?
    What were your reactions at the time and later?
    What were your physical reactions?
    What did you make of what you saw and experienced?
Normalization
    Comment on reactions – they are normal.
    Give anticipatory guidelines – explain what might be felt and what reactions can occur.
Future planning and coping
    Mobilize support. Ask what resources they have available at work and home. Who can help and what help do they need?
    Give advice on coping and on those who can help.
    What about family, children and work?

Disengagement
Any questions?
Explain possible development of symptoms.
They should decrease in near future.
If they persist for four weeks or more, they might need professional help.
Look for any loss of function or changes in ability at home, work or elsewhere.
Give a summary of what has happened in the debrief.
Do they want follow-up meetings? When and where?

Summary
The debriefer gives a brief summary of the session. Allow the group to disperse, but check any who might show particular symptoms of distress. These might be the result of the debrief or of deeper stress – or both.

Appendix B
NOTES FOR DEBRIEFERS

The debriefer should prepare a list of questions relevant to the situation and incident. The following open list gives general headings under which appropriate notes or questions can be listed.

Check-list for debriefers

Introduction
    Introduce self. Explain debriefing & explain rules.
    How did you learn about the event?
    What happened before it took place? Where were you?
Expectations and facts
    What did you expect to happen? What happened?
Thoughts
    What were your thoughts? What did you do and why?
Impressions
    What were/are your main impressions and memories?
    What did you see – hear – smell – touch – taste?
Emotions
    How did you feel at the time?
    What made you most upset? Did you cry?
Reactions
    How do you feel now?
Leaving
    What happened when you went home? How did wife and family react? What did others say that was helpful/unhelpful?
Normalization
    Explain normality of reactions to post trauma stress.
The Future
    What help do you and your family need now? What resources are available at work/home/elsewhere?
    Thank people for coming and taking part.

The questions under each section should be prepared beforehand and based on knowledge of what has happened. They must be appropriate and related to the particular incident and people involved. The questions asked in some cases will be very different from others.

For example, if you know you are to debrief after a car crash in which people were killed you would need to prepare different questions from those following an accident where nobody was killed. Also, the involvement of children and the deaths of children raises the possible level of response and reaction.

Examples

1   **A car accident with deaths**
Expectations and facts
   Did you expect to see dead bodies?
   How did you react to the bodies?
   Where did you find them and what did they look like?
   Did you expect the car to burst into flames?
   Did you try to rescue anybody? Why? Why not?
Thoughts
   What did you think when you saw the bodies?
   What do you think now?
   What did you think about most?
Impressions
   What were your main impressions of the bodies and injured?
   What smells? Burnt flesh, petrol, diesel oil?
   What sights? Charred bodies? Clothing, etc?
   What sounds? Screaming, shouting, moaning?
   What touch? Bodies, metal, glass?

2   **A violent bank robbery**
Expectations and facts
   What did the man look like when you first saw him?
   At first, what did you expect he wanted?
   When did you realize that it was a robbery?
   When did you first see the gun/weapon?
Thoughts
   What did you think when you saw he was wearing a hood/
   mask/carrying a gun?
   What did you think about being threatened?
Impressions
   What smells? Body sweat, fear, cordite, gun-oil?
   What sights? Weapons, violence, his eyes/mouth, etc?

What sounds? Shooting, shouting, screaming, threats?
What touch? By the gun? Were you hit/abused physically?
Emotions
Did you feel helpless, angry, afraid, violent, degraded?
Did you think you might be killed? When?
What did you feel about others involved? Women?
How do you feel now as a man/the manager?

You need to make the questions relevant to each unique situation.
If a child, spouse, relative or friend is involved, the questions
should be very sensitively thought out.

3   *An accident with the deaths of children*
Expectations and facts
Did you expect to see a dead child/children?
What did you do when you found the body?
What did it look like?
Thoughts
What did you think when you saw the *little* body?
What do you think might have been different if it had been an
adult?
Did you feel anger, sorrow, horror, injustice?
Impressions
What were your impressions of the scene which involved a dead
child?
What smells? Nappies, talcum, blood?
What sights? The little body, injuries, blood, toys?
What sounds? Crying, parents upset?
What touch? The body, clothing, toys?
Emotions
Did you cry? When and why?
What upset you most?
What were the reactions of others? Police, rescuers, parents,
friends, colleagues?

Similarly, the questions would be different for a suicide, murder,
minor accident, national disaster, shooting, hostage situation or a
war, or if the incident was sudden and unexpected or if people had
time to experience fear and terror for some time before the
incident took place.
The questions would also depend on who was being debriefed.

Men might be more defensive in answering questions about feelings than women or if other men are present. They might respond in a different manner if they are with close friends, family or colleagues.

Professional helpers or survivors who are being debriefed might ask other questions and have other concerns, especially about being involved and, perhaps, not being able to help.

Doctors. Their ability or inability to save life.

Clergy. Questions about meaning, purpose and faith.

Single people. Questions about the value of getting married or having children or seeing dead children.

Police. Questions about blame and responsibility.

Parents. When children are killed – questions about injustice and their responsibility and possible failure as parents. Survivors and helpers – identification with their own children. It might happen to them.

Helpers such as Fire and Rescue workers, nurses, ambulance personnel and many others might feel especially helpless and useless and express frustration, anger and rage.

The debriefing session should ensure that the model is adhered to and worked through and the questions should be asked in a sensitive manner, but those being debriefed should not be allowed to avoid the point of the questions.

Appendix C
TYPICAL EFFECTS OF
POST-TRAUMA STRESS
ON RELATIONSHIPS

- There can be changes in the way people see themselves, their wife, partner or children. Relationships can become very strained and difficult with lack of ability to communicate.
- If one person is suffering, they might not be able to talk to their partner and retreat behind a wall of silence or suppressed anger.
- Inability to stop talking about the event. This can become irritating and boring for others whose response might be to tell them to shut up and forget about it.
- Nightmares and dreams. Waking up in a panic or sweats. This can be very disturbing and frightening for partners also. Suddenly jumping out of bed.
- Feelings that life is a waste of time. 'What's the point?' Apathy. Partners can become angry about this.
- Inability to make even simple decisions. Loss of concentration. Disinterest in families, friends, hobbies. Others can wonder what this is about and become frustrated and angry.
- Feelings of vulnerability. Anxiety about the same things happening again. Confusion and disorientation. The response can be to tell them to pull themselves together.
- Pent-up feelings can result in anger and violence in the relationship, sometimes without any apparent cause. Shouting and remonstrating against anything or nothing.
- Loss of self-esteem or self-value and worth. 'I am useless. Why bother with anything?' Partners can respond by arguing or trying to convince them that this is not true and stress the value of their relationship, the family and home.
- Loss of interest in work or hobbies. Changing jobs. Wanting to move home. All cause upheaval in the family and seem so unnecessary to others.
- Looking for new relationships or partners. Dissatisfaction with present partner or family.
- Constant preoccupation with the incident. Keeping a diary of events or a scrapbook. This can be infuriating to others.

- Avoiding anything to do with the incident. Keeping away from people, including those who are there to help.
- A lack of understanding on the part of the person experiencing the incident of the effects of the incident or their behaviour on others in the family.
- Shame and fear about behaviour, especially of guilt or lack of ability to cope at the time and subsequently. 'I should have done this and I shouldn't be like this.'
- Feeling a complete failure. 'I did not do what I could or should have done. I did not behave like a man. I am even lower than an animal. I feel utterly degraded.'

Appendix D
THE STOCKHOLM SYNDROME

During a raid on a bank in Stockholm some people were held hostage by the robbers. Certain characteristics of the behaviour of both captors and captives were noticed and have occurred in similar hostage-taking incidents. These symptoms are known as The Stockholm Syndrome. Basically, the hostages develop feelings of sympathy and empathy with those who are holding them. Also, the captors develop sympathy with their prisoners. The characteristics are:

- *Blame* Those who are held hostage direct their anger and frustration at those in authority. They must have someone to blame – as in the similar reaction to bereavement. They might even blame others in the group of hostages.
- *Sympathy and empathy* The captives can come to believe that those who are holding them are not as bad as they first thought. They begin to see them as real human beings. Every little action of kindness shown to them is thought of as a sign that the captors must really be decent people. In a long-term hostage situation the release of one hostage is hailed with joy, and there is sometimes the feeling, 'Well they can't be all that bad can they? They have set someone free.' It seems not to matter that the captives were held for days, months or years. Similarly, the captors can develop close feelings and attachments to the hostages. In some cases, hostages have joined captors. It is likely that in many hostage situations the captors will distance themselves from the hostages in order to prevent this closeness from developing. It may be more difficult to cope with hostages when such a relationship has developed. Conversely, it might be advantageous to their cause for the captors to encourage such a relationship, especially if the captives begin to speak highly of them and criticize their own authorities. The political as well as personal implications of this are important. Hostage taking can be a powerful method of influencing individuals, groups or nations.

A number of people who were held hostage overseas said on their return that those who held them treated them well and they felt sympathy for their cause. While they had lost everything they possessed, many of them still seemed unable to hate their captors for what they had done. Much of their anger was turned against the British authorities at all levels both at home and in the country where they were held. This anger was still in evidence, and in some cases had deepened, two years later.

This is typical of 'The Stockholm Syndrome' and those who may be held hostage should be aware that such a relationship might develop. It can affect the relationships between those held hostage and their captors. On their return to freedom, it can continue to influence the way they think and feel about themselves, their fellow hostages and their captors. It will also affect relationships with their families and friends and in some measure determine how they survive and cope.

Index